Antique Golf Collectibles

IDENTIFICATION & VALUE GUIDE

- Clubs
- Balls
- Books
- Ceramics
- Metalwares
- Ephemera

Pete Georgiady

PHOTOGRAPHY BY
Richard Walker

COLLECTOR BOOKS

A Division of Schroeder Publishing Co., Inc.

Front cover (clockwise from center of page):
Gilt golf trophy of a man swinging a club and on wood base, in 1940s – 1950s attire, $60.00.
View of the face of an aluminum Huntly putter, 1920s, $150.00 – 200.00.
The Golfer's Pocket Tip Book, 1911, $35.00.
Two carrot-shaped wooden golf tees, each $3.00.
Old dimple ball, circa 1920, $5.00.
Burke Golf Co. Columbia Special niblick with dash face scoring, 1925, $35.00.
Back cover (clockwise from top):
The Manhattan Tee, black rubber, patented 1915, $75.00.
Wooden peg tee with rubber top, a replica of the Grant 1899 patent, $25.00.
MacGregor Master 30 driver with mother-of-pearl crown inlay, early 1930s, $200.00 – 300.00.
"Major" model slotted-head niblick from the series of Brown's Perforated Irons, 1908, $2,500.00 – 5,000.00.
Burbank brand golf ball, early 1930s, $600.00.
Nancy comic book with golf theme cover, 1960s, $20.00.
Golf for the Late Beginner, by Henry Hughes, 1911, $30.00.
Silver charm in the shape of a golf bag containing clubs, for either bracelet or pendant, 1930s, $80.00.

In the center:
Lady's silver pin in the shape of a golf green with flagstick in hole, 1930s, $75.00.
Lady's silver pin made of two small golf clubs and ball, 1920s, $100.00.

Cover design by Beth Summers
Book design by Barry Buchanan
Photography by Richard Walker

COLLECTOR BOOKS
P.O. Box 3009
Paducah, Kentucky 42002-3009

www.collectorbooks.com

Copyright © 2006 Pete Georgiady

The current values in this book should be used only as a guide. They are not
intended to set prices, which vary from one section of the country to another.
Auction prices as well as dealer prices vary greatly and are affected by condition
as well as demand. Neither the authors nor the publisher assumes responsibility
for any losses that might be incurred as a result of consulting this guide.

Searching for a Publisher?

We are always looking for knowledgeable people considered to be experts within their fields. If you feel that there is a real need for a book on your collectible subject and have a large comprehensive collection, contact Collector Books.

Proudly printed and bound in the
United States of America

CONTENTS

ACKNOWLEDGMENTS

The items pictured in this book were photographed in the collections of the following individuals who graciously allowed their use:

David Berkowitz
Palatine, Illinois

Andrew Crewe
Springfield, Ohio

Jack Dezieck
Great Barrington, Massachusetts

Chuck Furjanic
Dallas, Texas

Greg & Barbara Hall
Bay Village, Ohio

John Miller
Cooperstown, New York

Ron Stewart
Queensbury, New York

Dr. Gary Wiren
North Palm Beach, Florida
*The photographers, Richard and
Elizabeth Walker, would especially like to
thank Dr. Wiren, whose hospitality in allowing
us to photograph his extensive collection
in large part made this book possible.*

Interested in joining?

Golf Collectors' Society
PO Box 3103
Ponte Vedra Beach, FL 32004-3103
www.golfcollectors.com
(904) 825-2191

British Golf Collectors Society
20 Druim Avenue
Inverness, IV2 4LG
Scotland
taormina@btinternet.com
01463-231145

One of Wilson's top models was this Gene Sarazen autograph driver with ivorine face insert and back weight (imitation ivory). A professionally refinished club is the standard now. Original finish is highly desirable but almost impossible to find seventy years after this club was introduced. $100.00.

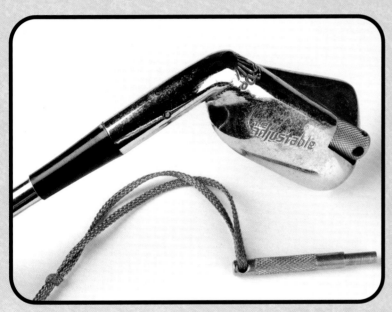

This adjustable iron was made, circa 1950, for the person who wanted to walk the course and carry only a single club. The lofts range from zero degrees for putting to the wedge angle for high approaches. Adjustable irons have been made for over 100 years, but the main reason for their lack of success is that while the loft of the blade can be changed, the length of the shaft is constant, as is the lie of the head, very awkward for putting and the wedge-type shots. Marked only "The Adjustable." The rod-shaped key, used to loosen the knurled screw that locks the blade angle, is frequently missing, lowering the value. $75.00.

One of the true classic clubs of the game, the Spalding Cash-In putter was a huge seller for over 30 years. Many versions were produced, but an early one, like this, with the coated shaft, is hard to find. $200.00.

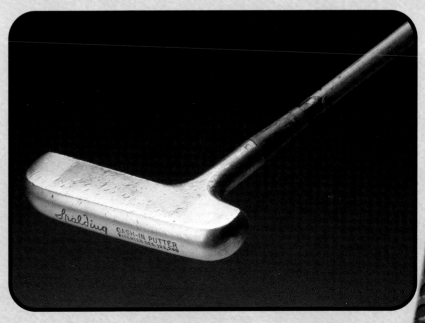

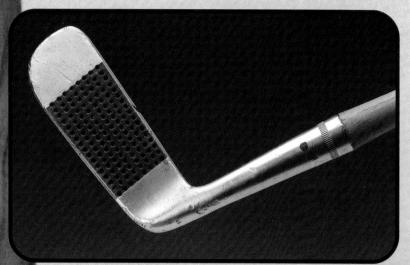

The Wilson Mark Harris Perfect Balance putter is a good example of how a few putters were still made with wood shafts after steel-shafted woods and irons had replaced hickory-shafted clubs. $50.00.

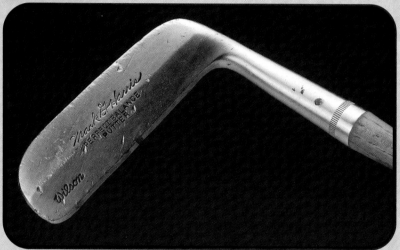

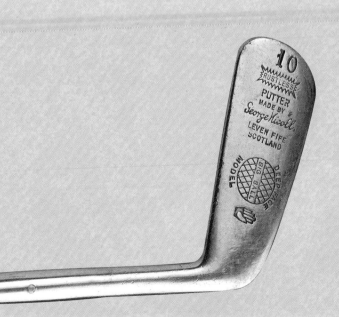

This putter is one of the first from the George Nicoll Company, Leven, Scotland, to come with a steel shaft. The Big Ball model was introduced in the early 1930s, and since steel shafts were legalized for use in Britain in 1929, Big Ball irons can be found with either wood or metal shafts. Putter with wood shaft, $40.00; putter with steel shaft, $25.00.

Sam Buckley was one of Henley's American sales agents, from the looks of this 1898 ad.

Sold by all Dealers
or
Sam'l Buckley & Co.,
100 William Street, New York.

Many guttie balls came in a six-pole, or six-panel, configuration. This five-panel Diamond ball was patented in January 1899, had a diamond pattern, and was manufactured by Whit and Barnes, Akron, Ohio. $850.00.

The Diamond ball, showing its unique marking, in a 1900 ad from (US) *Golf* magazine.

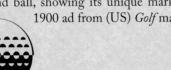

We make the *celebrated*
Diamond and Norka Golf Balls

All balls made from selected Gutta-Percha and thoroughly seasoned. Try them and you will use them.

THE WHITMAN & BARNES MFG. CO.
AKRON, OHIO
Branch Houses:
NEW YORK, N. Y.   SYRACUSE, N. Y.
CINCINNATI, O.   CHICAGO, ILL.   KANSAS CITY, MO.
ST. CATHARINES, ONT.   LONDON, ENG.

Also sole manufacturers of the famous
Willie Dunn's Stars and Stripes

Only an X-ray may be able to determine whether this ball is a solid guttie or a rubber-core ball with an early guttie cover. Thornton's, the retail store in Edinburgh and Glasgow, was selling golf goods early in the 1890s, at a time guttie balls were in use exclusively. The large bramble bumps are uncommon. $600.00.

Marked "Murton's Tyne," this bramble guttie was sold by the sports shop named Murton in the northern English city of Newcastle upon Tyne. $450.00.

The bramble pattern was one of reverse (outward) dimple marks. These two guttie brands from *Golfing* magazine, 1902, show that the rubber core balls hadn't yet taken over the entire market.

Cochrane's of Edinburgh made The Albert in several cover patterns over time. This square dimple pattern appeared around 1920. $250.00.

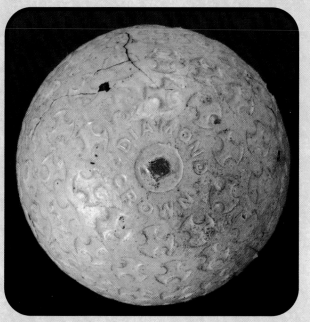

The fancier the shape of the dimples, the more collectible the ball may be. This Diamond Crown from Worthington has a unique three-armed indentation. $450.00.

Introduced in 1913, the Worthington Ring featured a pattern of diamonds inside large dish-shaped dimples. $400.00.

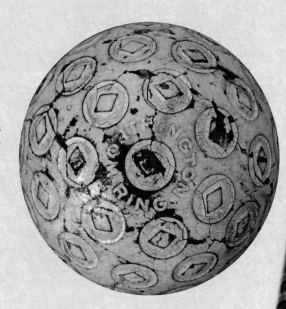

Collecting Golf Balls
Early Rubber-Core Balls

The inverted, or perhaps raised, dimple marks on this Worthington White easily lost their paint, giving the ball a two-color look. $450.00.

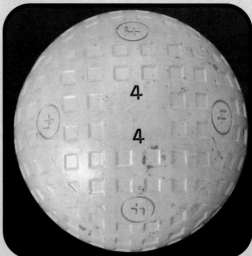

The 4-ball-in-mesh pattern was made by Worthington before World War One. $35.00.

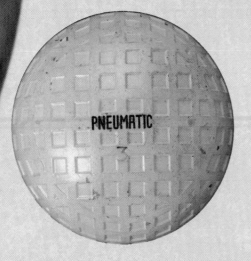

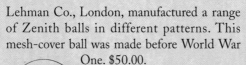

The Pneumatic from Goodyear Rubber, Akron, Ohio, was only one of several pneumatic balls that utilized trapped air in the centers to create liveliness. The Goodyear Pneumatic with the mesh cover was brought out in 1905. $1,500.00.

Lehman Co., London, manufactured a range of Zenith balls in different patterns. This mesh-cover ball was made before World War One. $50.00.

The St. Mungo Manufacturing Company of Glasgow, Scotland, produced over 60 ball types using the Colonel name over a 40-year span. There were Arch Colonels, Blue Colonels, Red Colonels, Pro Colonels, and White Colonels — and scores of others in a variety of cover patterns. A collector wishing to specialize could easily devote an entire collection to nothing but Colonel brand balls. Although it was a British company, St. Mungo became a stateside manufacturer when it bought the Kempshall Golf Company of Arlington, New Jersey, around 1910. So, collectors can find Colonel balls on either side of the Atlantic.

This tidy display of 20 Colonel balls, each different, illustrates the diversity of St. Mungo's products. Besides the balls, other St. Mungo items, like print advertising from period golf magazines and ball boxes like the American-made Arch Colonel box shown here, are collectible. Box, $400.00.

Another highly singular dimple design is the double crescent moon on the Arch Colonel from the St. Mungo Company, Glasgow. $350.00.

Also sporting a double crescent, but with additional lines of square dimples, is this Colonel Practice ball from St. Mungo. $150.00.

A Colonel ad from (British) *Golf Illustrated*, 1910.

The maker of this Watson's ball is not known. The big dimples with the bisecting lines appear on no other ball. $1,000.00.

Nothing is known about this ball marked only with "L." However, the ball is old, perhaps 1910 – 1915, and has uncommonly large dish-shaped dimples. $100.00.

The maker of this ball is not known, and the only marking is "RGD 343103," which is probably the design registration number for the three-dimple cluster. $250.00.

This St. Nicholas ball features a square-in-a-circle dimple mark. The ball is from the early part of the twentieth century, but the maker is not now known. $400.00.

This ball with the triple-line latticework or British Union Jack flag marking is a Henley ball from England, circa 1915. $450.00.

Made by the North British Rubber Company, the Clincher Cross in bramble pattern (and large 29 size) was used up until the First World War. $450.00.

The Goodrich Rubber Company, Akron, Ohio, made its Goodrich Whippet brand ball around 1912. Its unique triangle dimple made it a visually attractive ball. $350.00.

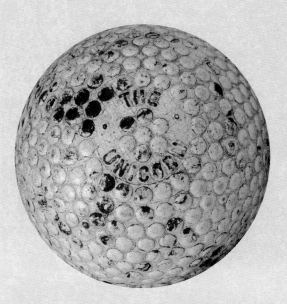

The Unicorn had a typical bramble-type cover, but it is uncertain who produced this brand. $200.00.

The Faroid ball had concentric circular ridges as a cover pattern. The ball had to be teed in such a way that the club had to strike a target point of impact. $6,500.00.

This ringed pattern ball looks similar to a Faroid but has no name. $3,500.00.

Unique, historical, and scarce, the Henry's Rifled Ball is desired by every ball collector. This ball was first sold in 1903, and the cover has swirled ridges resembling the rifling in a gun barrel. The idea was that the rifling would make the ball spin in the air like a bullet for greater accuracy. The theoretical principle never came close to real world golf aeronautical physics. However, this ball clearly says "Henley's," so perhaps Henley acquired the manufacturing rights from Mr. Henry, who was a gun maker by trade, not a part of any golfing concern. $20,000.00.

This 1904 ad for the Henry's Rifled Ball shows that Alexander Henry was a gun maker.

Britain's involvement in World War I virtually shut down the golf industry. The biggest blow was to the manpower — professionals and golf manufacturing workers alike went to the front and many never returned. But the years between the two World Wars saw meteoric growth in golf in America and Great Britain.

The biggest change came in the 1930s when, over time, the round dimple pattern replaced all other cover patterns and became the standard. It might have been good for golfers, but it made collecting balls more boring. From then onward, the markings — the name, logo, signature, or other distinguishing marks — became the differentiators, since cover patterns had become so homogenous.

Harlequin brand balls, from the Game Ball Company, London, were sold in the 1920s. Any ball made before the Second World War that is still in its original paper or box is highly desirable. Harlequin with wrapper, $250.00; without wrapper, $50.00.

This Harlequin, by the Game Balls Co., has a variation of the stretch mesh pattern. $45.00.

The Harlequin Super 4 was one of the several names used in the Harlequin mesh-cover series. $40.00.

This Harlequin Super 3 has a different sort of mesh scheme, with the individual platelets looking like big square doughnuts. $100.00.

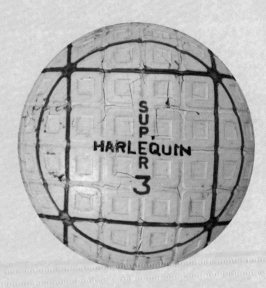

One of the most popular balls sold in Britain, the Dunlop 65 (or Sixty Five) came in both American and British sizes. This ball in original black wrapper is the 1.68" American size. $50.00.

The PGA of America used the buying power of its large membership to get volume prices on clubs and PGA brand balls. It would then offer member professionals those items at affordable prices, prices lower than a single pro could negotiate with a manufacturer. Several makers supplied balls to the PGA for resale. This unique 6-pole mesh pattern is attractive, but the ball maker remains unknown. $600.00.

The Great Scot, dimple ball from the 1930s. $15.00.

The Swan brand ball from Charles Rodwell Company, London. $15.00.

A dimple ball simply called Whiz, produced by B. F. Goodrich in America. $25.00.

Pluto was a devil-like symbol of the underworld and also the trademark of the French Lick resort in Indiana. The Pluto mark was used on clubs by A. G. Lockwood, the professional at French Lick. This ball has a mesh cover pattern. $75.00.

The mesh cover of this ball carried both brand name spellings — *Peau-Deau* and *Po-Do*. The brand was carried by the Walgreens retail chain in the 1930s. $35.00.

The Penfold LL was introduced in 1934. Its lattice pattern was unique. Penfold was a British company; "USA" meant this ball was made in the larger size for the American market. $150.00.

In the 1930s, General Electric got into the golf business, making Schavolite golf clubs — drivers with a matrix of cloth scraps and an epoxy-type resin. These dimple balls were manufactured to go with the clubs in retail stores. $25.00.

The maker of this Flight Commander mesh-cover ball is unknown. $25.00.

The Davega store had one of the largest golf equipment selections in New York City in the 1920s. This mesh-pattern ball was from its store line. $25.00.

There was no mistaking the size of this ball. Made by Thomas E. Wilson of Chicago, the Official Standard 1.62 dimple ball was used by golfers in the 1920s. $20.00.

The Maxim mesh was made by the W. F. Fisher Co., Brighton, England, in the 1920s. $25.00.

The Maxim dimple eventually replaced the mesh pattern. $15.00.

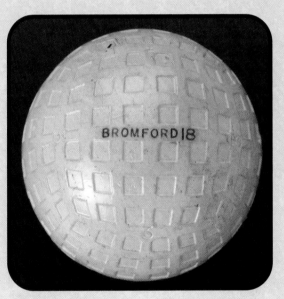

The Bromford mesh came from the Golf Ball Development Co. in the 1920s. $25.00.

Grand Prize was a highly successful line of upper-end clubs from Burke Golf Co. of Newark, Ohio. This brand of mesh balls was sold to go with the clubs. $35.00.

Another mesh-cover ball from Burke in the 1920s was the 50-50 model. $35.00.

The Kinesthetic Process Co., Long Island, New York, was a company that reprocessed old golf balls. Tungsten was one of their trade marked names. This mesh cover dates from the mid 1920s. $45.00.

The North British Rubber Company, Edinburgh, Scotland made the North British line of golf balls for many years. This stretched mesh cover ball dates from the early 1930s. $25.00.

The Bonnie Brook mesh-cover ball came from a maker presently unknown. $25.00.

The Ashbourne with a dimple cover comes from an unknown maker. The firm of Foster Brothers made golf clubs in the town of Ashbourne, and perhaps this is part of its product line. $15.00.

A stretched mesh cover marked "Forgan," from the legendary firm of Robert Forgan & Son, St. Andrews. $50.00.

Made by Dunlop, the Warwick model was a popular seller for several decades. In this version, the cover is an interesting mix of square and round dimples. $75.00.

A stretched-mesh-cover ball marked "Cotton." There is no documentation to suggest it, but possibly this ball could have come from the shop of future Open Champion Henry Cotton, maybe when he was at Langley Park in the late 1920s. $45.00.

Both Spalding and Dunlop made balls named Nimble; however, these two probably came from a different maker altogether. The mesh pattern is unique; the dimples come in a variety of shapes — four, five, and six sided. $100.00.

A simple dimple-cover ball. The Red Flash trade name belonged to the Wannamaker Department Store of New York, Philadelphia, and other East Coast cities. $15.00.

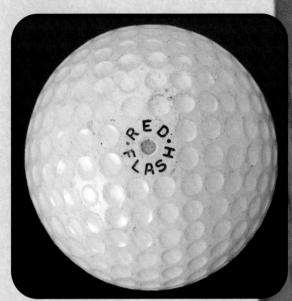

The 75 model sold by Penfold in the 1930s had a standard mesh cover. $25.00.

The A.J. Reach Company of Philadelphia was a large supplier of golf items, both for the proprietary Reach brand and under the Spalding name, the Reach owner. This standard dimple ball with the Reach name was sold in the 1930s. $15.00.

The Dunlop Company put out
The Dunhill dimple ball in the
1920s. $15.00.

There were countless ball manufacturers. The little-
known Harned Golf Company produced its brand
of ball with the H-arrow logo in the
1930s. $25.00.

This mesh-cover ball marked "Winged Foot" probably
was privately branded for the Winged
Foot Golf Club in Westchester
County, NY. $75.00.

This unusual pattern of triangle-shaped dimples came from the Silvertown Company of London. Several styles of Lynx brand ball were made, with these two having one of the more unusual covers. $200.00.

Like most of the other large club manufacturers, the Kroydon Golf Company made branded balls to sell with its clubs. The mesh-cover Kroydon Red Star — even though the color of this sleeve of balls was blue — was a top-line ball. $45.00.

The mesh-cover Western (Star) ball came from an unknown maker. $40.00.

The White Colonel in the bramble cover was one of several dozen ball styles in the Colonel name and made by the St. Mungo Manufacturing Co. The various St. Mungo Colonels were large-selling balls. $65.00.

The Canada Golf Ball Company of Toronto was the only golf ball manufacturing company in Canada in the 1920s. This +4 model had a mesh-type cover with three sections instead of the usual four or six. $60.00.

The England LL ball, with its lattice-mesh cover, was made by Dunlop in the 1920s. $65.00.

Wannamaker's also sold a brand of ball called The Wonder Ball. Its cover pattern was diamond-shaped dimples, and it is very collectible today. $300.00.

The Worthington Company made this impressive-looking ball called the Long Flash. Not only does it have an interesting stretch-mesh cover, but the large, pointed color pips are visually arresting. $250.00.

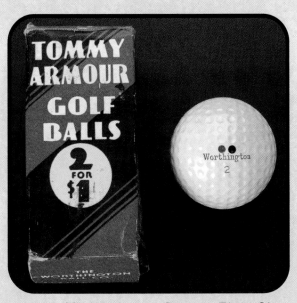

The Worthington Company, Elyria, Ohio, made these Tommy Armour brand balls in the 1930s. The balls themselves are worth $5.00 – 10.00 each, and the box is worth $50.00.

The maker of the Cambridge brand ball is unknown at this time, but was probably English. The brickwork mesh pattern is unusual and scarce. $125.00.

The Radius C3 ball was so named because the ribs of its mesh pattern were radiused, or rounded, instead of having hard edges like those on other mesh-cover balls. $50.00.

The LAV monogram on this ball stands for Von Lengerke & Antoine, a Chicago retail store that sold a large volume of golf equipment, much of it privately branded for V.L.&A. The dimple pattern has been called sand dollar or star-in-circle. $400.00.

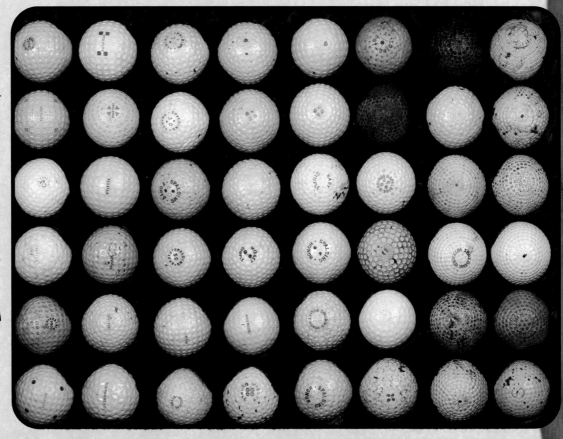

Here are two display trays, each with 48 balls. This collection represents just a handful of the hundreds of brands made by Spalding over the last century. In the first tray, some of the older bramble-pattern balls from the turn of the century and first decade of the 1900s share space with a few mesh-cover balls and many early dimple balls.

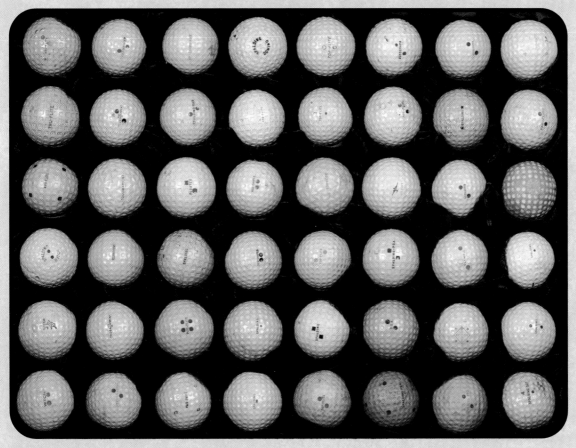

In the second tray, several of the balls have fancy covers or mesh markings, but most are regular dimple balls from the 1940s and 1950s. Balls of this vintage can still be found in the pockets of old golf bags, at flea markets, at swap meets, and at collectibles shows, and can be purchased for $1.00 or less.

The post–World War II era created two new groups of balls for collectors. Signature balls feature the autographs of famous golf professionals endorsing manufacturers' equipment lines. The second category is logo balls with markings that include everything from the presidential seal to major golf tournament souvenir scenes to local dairy company logos.

One of the last balls to be made with a mesh cover was the U.S. Rubber Company's True Blue model. This ball was sold in the 1950s, and the "electronic" branding must have been an impressive attribute. $20.00.

With the logo of the astronaut, this ball commemorates Alan Shepherd's famous 1971 scientific experiment of hitting a golf ball on the moon. $100.00.

President George Bush, following a precedent set by others before him, has special balls made with the presidential seal and his signature. Most are given as gifts to friends, politicians, and visitors. Some are actually used on the golf course by the chief executive. $80.00.

The president is not the only national executive to have personalized golf balls. Vice presidents play golf, too. Here's a pretty simple stamp for the former VP Spiro T. Agnew, Richard Nixon's running mate. This particular ball was a novelty item and not the property of the vice president. It also has a caricature of Agnew on the reverse side. $20.00.

A recent vice president who is an avid golfer is Dan Quayle of Indiana. His ball features the seal of his office and his autograph. $50.00.

A souvenir logo ball from the 1997 Ryder Cup played in Valderrama, Spain. $10.00.

During the First World War, when the supply of rubber was diverted to the war effort, balls were made of wood. Because the ball was susceptible to splitting when hit with the grain, a dot was placed in the spot against the grain where the ball was to be struck. $200.00.

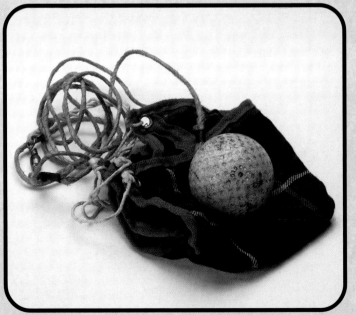

The parachute ball was a novel practice device from the early twentieth century. It usually consisted of a regular golf ball with a cloth parachute attached. When the ball was hit off the tee, the chute would prevent it from traveling hundreds of yards. $250.00.

Practice balls have always been a study in materials. The object is to shorten the distance the practice ball travels so the golfer practicing doesn't have to walk hundreds of yards to retrieve it. This Practo brand woolen knit ball is typical of early twentieth century practice balls. The red color was meant to assist in locating it. Knit balls were popular until the 1960s, when plastic became more economical. $50.00.

Knit practice balls were marketed in this 1931 ad from *American Golfer* magazine.

25¢ EACH *at All Stores*

Hundreds of thousands of golfers, beginners as well as experts, know by actual use that Practo improves their game. Right weight, right size, right feel. Does no indoor damage. The world's biggest seller. Most stores have them.

Patented and manufactured by

RELIABLE KNITTING WORKS

2030 W. Lloyd Street Milwaukee, Wis.

Practo KNITTED GOLF BALL

THE PRACTICE BALL LEADING GOLFERS USE

$1 SEND FOR BOX OF FOUR If your dealer cannot supply you. RELIABLE KNITTING WORKS 2030 W. Lloyd St., Milwaukee, Wis., Dept. G.

Gentlemen: Please send me a box of 4 Practo. I am sending $1 enclosed.

Name.................
Address..............
City..................

Many novice collectors mistakenly take a ball like this to be an old golf feather ball. More likely, it is an English "fives" ball, fives being an outdoor game played like very rudimentary baseball. Fives balls have four pieces of leather in their covers, shaped like watermelon slices. The covers of real golf feather balls are made of three pieces of hide with hidden seams. $25.00.

The part of ball collecting that features the artistic side of the discipline is the collection of the boxes in which the balls were packaged. For more than a century, balls have been packaged in boxes of twelve. There are exceptions, but for the most part, the dozen has been the unit of measure.

Artwork on the lids of the boxes varies from plain lettering to multicolor illustrations. Like many other collectible items, ball boxes are collectible and valuable today because they were considered trash in their day and readily discarded. When the balls were removed from the box, it was rarely used to store balls. Pencils or bits of paper, maybe, but rarely balls.

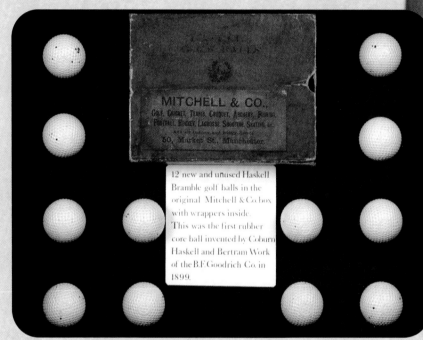

This is a one-of-a-kind find: an original Haskell box, with an additional label affixed to the lid for Mitchell & Co., a sports depot in Manchester, England, and containing a dozen unused Haskell patent bramble balls. Finding just one mint Haskell ball is good fortune. Finding 12 at once is an unbelievable feat. $30,000.00.

Most ball boxes come in a shape that is almost square so the balls can be arranged in four rows of three-ball sleeves. This Haskell box from the early 1900s is more linear, and the balls were arranged in two long rows of six balls each. Long boxes like this, for Haskell Match golf balls, are very rare. $300.00.

Another long box for Haskell-Whiz golf balls from before 1910. $300.00.

The Brig o' Doon, made famous by Robert Burns, is pictured on the lid of this box for Doon brand golf balls. From the turn of the century, the box is well worn with some seams opening, but the cover artwork is intact, bright, and artistic. $250.00.

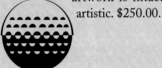

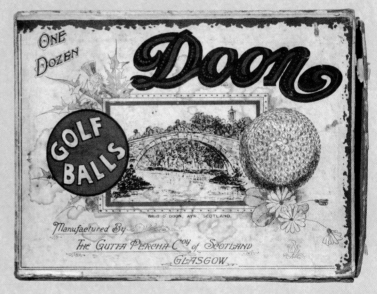

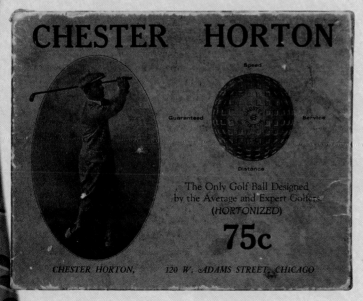

A photo on the lid of this box of the young Chester Horton was probably taken years before these balls were manufactured in the 1920s. Horton was a well-known professional and instructor who spent most of his career in the Chicago area. $250.00.

There are two interesting items to note on this Silvertown box from the late 1890s. The first is that, besides the London addresses for warehouses and works, there are two addresses for locations in France, a place where golf was played but never in a large way. The other is the use of the legends "guaranteed made from new material" and "thoroughly seasoned." "New material" meant that the balls were not remolded gutties, and the "seasoned" remark reminds us that guttie balls needed to sit for a while and cure after they were manufactured, in order to harden and solidify. $500.00.

The Silvertown Company also made balls under the Silver King name. This 1920s vintage box shows the mesh-cover, blue-dot model. $175.00.

A fancier Silver King box also showing the famous Silver King golf man, the company's trademark. The artwork helps make this box more collectible than one with just lettering on the cover. $275.00.

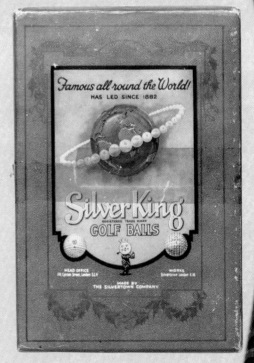

175

One of the later Silvertown brands was the Silver Duke from the 1930s. While colorful and over 70 years old, it does not have as much artistic value as the older boxes. $50.00.

This very elegant-looking Dunlop box from the 1920s may well have been a special Christmas season presentation box. $250.00.

These two Dunlop Maxfli boxes, once containing mesh-cover balls, illustrate some of the subtle differences in branding. The balls are basically the same, yet one came in a black marking and the other in a blue marking. There is some fraying on the sides and spots where the cardboard panels are separating, but the cover artwork is intact and colorful. $150.00 each.

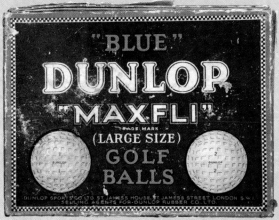

MacGregor Clan brand golf balls with two Scottie dogs. The 25¢ price for individual balls indicates the brand for this box dates from the 1940s. $65.00.

Spalding has made balls for the British market for a century. The Top-Flite brand was one of their strongest sellers. This box held British size mesh cover balls. $50.00.

These Spiro T. Agnew balls were more novelty items than pro-line balls. A caricature of the veep was imprinted on each ball. Box, $15.00; box with 12 balls, $60.00.

Undoubtedly a Christmas season promotional item, this plastic snowman contains three Dunlop Golf Cup golf balls. $40.00.

A box of mint, still-in-wrapper Dunlop 65 golf balls from the 1960s. $100.00, especially if found in the British 1.62 size, no longer in production.

From the 1950s, GBD brand balls came in a colorful but ordinary box. For collectibles information, it is always a plus to have an image of the ball on the cover so that years hence, collectors will know what the ball looked like. $20.00.

There was golf for several hundred years before there were true golf tees as we know them. Up until 1920, it was commonplace for a golfer to tee his ball on the teeing ground with a small mound of moist sand. It was only after WWI that the ubiquitous wooden peg tee came into favor.

Before that, there were small molds for making sand tees. Several inventors designed both platform tees that rested on top of the turf and disposable tees made from paper.

The variety of tee types, shapes, and materials is extremely broad. Most tees are pretty inexpensive, and only the sand tee molds from the nineteenth century present higher prices for acquisition.

Bakelite sand mold for making a sand tee. Moist sand was pressed into the cup, the open end of the tee was placed on the ground, and when the plunger was pressed the sand was ejected from the cup. This was one of the last sand tee molds sold; it was patented in 1928. $100.00.

The Anchor Tee had a rubber tee mount attached by string to a heavy metal anchor weight. Patented in 1900. $200.00.

183

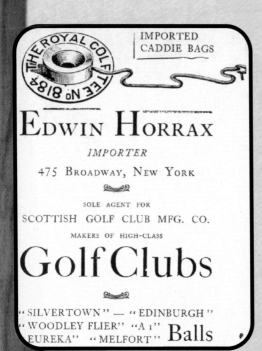

EDWIN HORRAX
IMPORTER
475 BROADWAY, NEW YORK

SOLE AGENT FOR
SCOTTISH GOLF CLUB MFG. CO.
MAKERS OF HIGH-CLASS
Golf Clubs

"SILVERTOWN" — "EDINBURGH"
"WOODLEY FLIER" "A 1"
"EUREKA" "MELFORT" Balls

Similar to the Anchor Tee, the Royal Golf Tee, sold in the Horrax store, also had a tether to prevent it from sailing off when the ball was struck. This ad is taken from an 1898 (US) *Golf* magazine.

Conical paper tees were inexpensive to make and use.

The Senat patent tee (top row, right) had a numeric scale for calibrating height. Its patent was the first United States patent issued for a golf tee, 1896. $75.00.

One of the most popular tees was the Tufts Tee (top row, center), circa 1930. $30.00.

Paper tees were ideal vehicles for advertising. The Auditorium Garage probably gave these out with parking garage tickets as a promotion. $25.00.

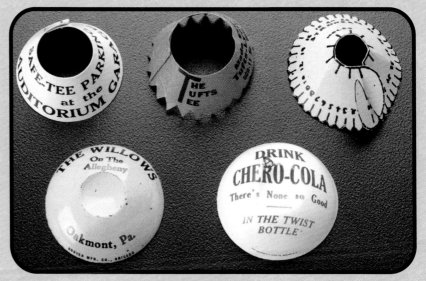

Hemispherical stamped metal tees, especially those carrying advertising messages, were popular in the 1927 – 1935 time frame. The two shown here promoted a hotel and a soft drink. $35.00 each.

The conical paper tee idea was rekindled recently with the Launch Tee. $5.00.

TEES

The Stay-Put is a modern version of the older Angle Tee, which was inserted in the ground at an angle and pointed in the direction of ball flight. They were subsequently deemed nonconforming by the USGA. $10.00.

Golf tees were commonly sold in small cloth sacks containing 50 or 100 tees. This sack full came from the London sporting goods company J.B. Halley. $75.00.

A panoply of yellow tees from eight decades of the peg tee. Shapes include:

Trumpet (far left)
Carrot (second from left)
Goblet (bottom left and far right)
    Classic (second and third from right)
    Funnel (top right)
    The original Reddy tee (bottom right)

Individually, these tees cost 25¢ to $1.00 each.

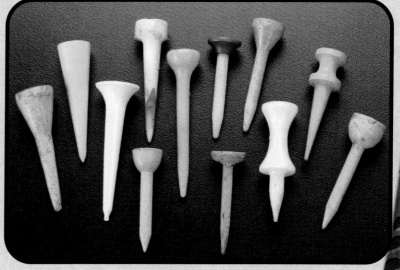

Collectors will have more luck finding individual tees than original tee boxes, which are highly collectible. The three here date from the 1930s. Range, $75.00 – 125.00.

Rex tees were made of zinc, not wood. Even if there are only a few tees remaining in the box, the box value goes up. Marketed in 1926. $150.00 for box with tees.

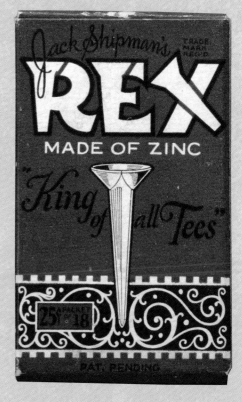

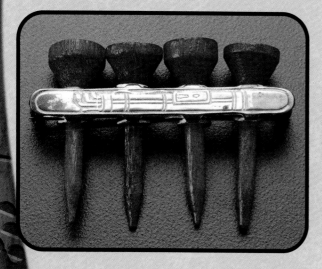

Tee holders come in a wide variety of shapes and with a wide variety of fasteners. This holder of four funnel tees has a pin fastener, and the holding bar is stamped to look like a golf bag. $40.00.

This tee holder for four goblet tees is made from plastic and has a clip-on arrangement for a golf bag. The front was also a good vehicle for advertising or promotion. $25.00.

H. EARL CLACK CO.

Leather holders usually had loops on the back for attaching them to belts on golf bags. One holds five goblet tees, the other holds six red plastic trumpet tees, probably replacements. Circa 1930. Each holder, $50.00.

This pin-fastened holder of four Red Head brand tees has a decorative button in front with the likeness of an Airedale terrier. $60.00.

A leather golf tee carrying case with loops for 10 tees. It probably attached to a golf bag. $15.00.

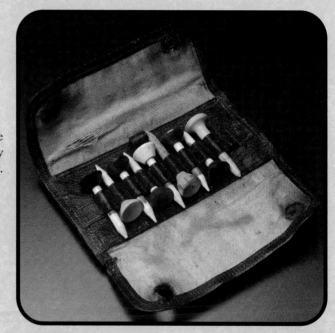

Five unusual tees, left to right: The TNT, made to look like a short stick of dynamite with fuse, circa 1925, $50.00; a two-piece metal tee — a copper stem topped with a silver cup, $35.00; Old Crow tee, from the distiller of the whiskey sharing that name, circa 1960, $30.00; red plastic carrot-shaped tee, $5.00; gilt naked lady tee, $25.00.

TEES

Six metal and plastic tees, left to right: silver metal goblet tee, $60.00; Rex brand zinc tee, $25.00; aluminum tee, $10.00; polished mahogany tee with brass tip, $15.00; slender clear plastic tee, $5.00; purple aluminum tee with rubber bumper to protect club face, $20.00.

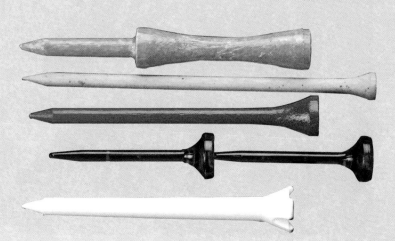

Extra high tees, top to bottom: classical shape, $5.00; ultrathin wooden tee, $3.00; standard trumpet shape, $1.00; double-height plastic, $3.00; white plastic with crown top, $3.00.

Spring-top extraheight tees that bend at impact, then snap back. Each has a tether with an anchor device for retrieval, in case the tee travels when hit. $10.00 each.

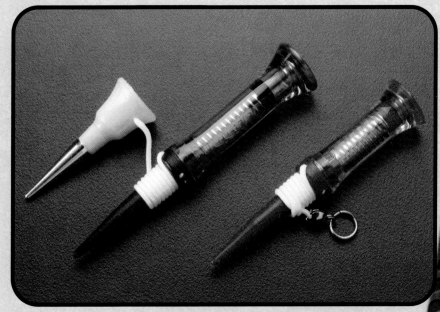

TEES

A plastic, two-piece adjustable height tee with brush-type ball cup. The clear plastic portion is placed in the ground and the red portion can be adjusted to the proper height. $10.00.

Two different heights of plastic, brush-top tees with rubber bumpers. The taller would be for tee shots with a driver, the shorter for irons. The two are tethered for loss prevention. $10.00 (pair).

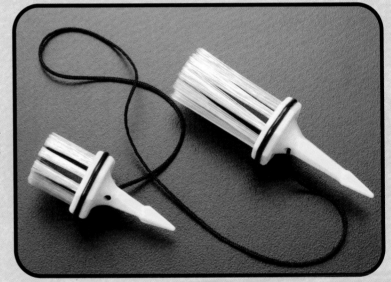

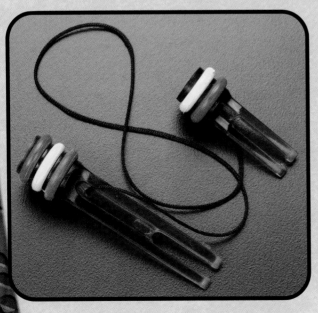

A similar set of different height plastic tees, one with two bumpers, the taller tee with three. $10.00.

GOLF BOOKS

"Golf book collectors are twice blessed. They love the grandest game of all…and they love books."

After collectors of golf clubs and balls, the next largest group of specialists is the collectors of golf books. Writers have found an inexhaustible supply of golf stuff to write about, starting with the first "book" about golf, a mid-eighteenth century poem in booklet form titled "The Goff." There were several editions, and copies often sell for over $25,000 each.

Golf's foremost bibliographer, Richard Donovan, estimates there are over 15,000 golf books, and they are listed in his latest edition of *The Game of Golf and the Printed Word.* That ought to keep prospective collectors busy for a while.

Golf books fall into several categories, which helps collectors specialize even more. Most are books of golf instruction — everyone wants to learn to be a better golfer, and there are dozens of people, golf professionals and otherwise, who feel they can teach you through an instruction book. There are also books containing golf fiction, essays about golf, history, humor, biographies, and information about equipment, course architecture, course maintenance, and rules. The books shown here are chosen from the 15,000 available because they have colorful or distinct covers.

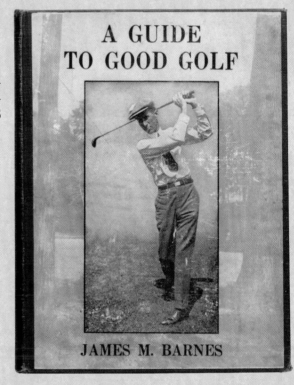

Barnes, James: *A Guide to Good Golf.* Golf instruction from the winner of the first American PGA Championship and 1921 US Open, 1925. $25.00.

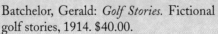

Batchelor, Gerald: *Golf Stories.* Fictional golf stories, 1914. $40.00.

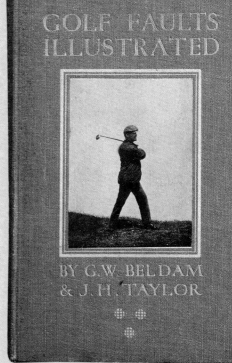

Bedlam, George W., and Taylor, J. H.: *Golf Faults Illustrated*. Instructional book concentrating on correcting faults, 1905. $45.00.

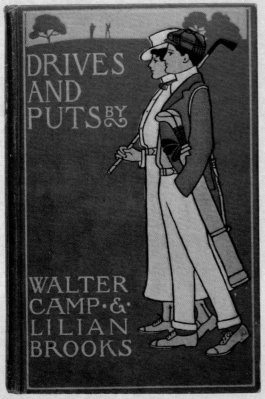

Camp, Walter, and Brooks, Lilian: *Drives & Puts*. Fictional stories from 1899. $150.00.

Clay, Bertha: *Her Only Sin*. A dimestore novel with no relevance to golf but a lovely golf-themed illustration on the cover, 1926. $10.00.

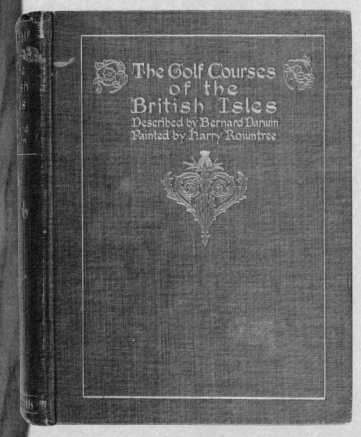

Darwin, Bernard, and Rowntree, Harry: *Golf Courses of the British Isles*. A survey of the more famous courses in Britain and Ireland. Descriptions written by the inimitable Darwin; the artwork is painted by Rowntree. $1,250.00.

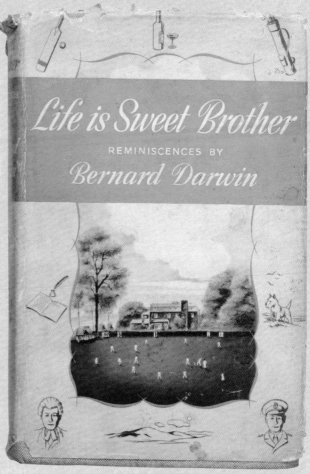

Darwin, Bernard: *Life is Sweet Brother*. Reminiscences from the great British writer, 1940. $35.00.

Dunn, John Duncan, and Jessup, Elon: *Intimate Golf Talks*. Instruction from Willie Dunn's nephew, 1920. $45.00.

Hecker, Genevieve: *Golf for Women*. Instruction for women learning the new game, 1902. $125.00.

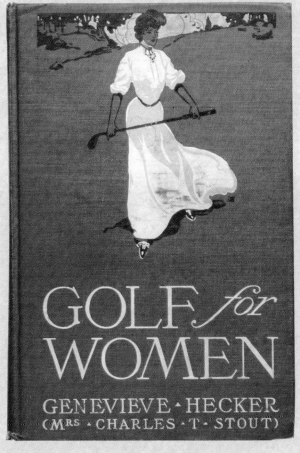

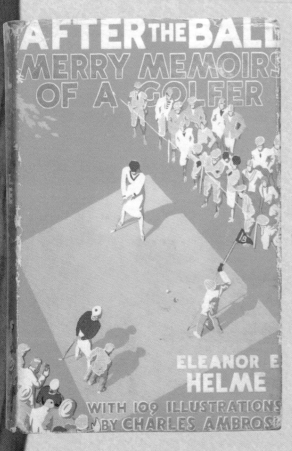

Helme, Eleanor E.: *After the Ball.* Stories and anecdotes from her career, 1925. $35.00.

Hughes, Henry: *Golf for the Late Beginner.* An instructional book for those learning golf late in life, 1911. $30.00.

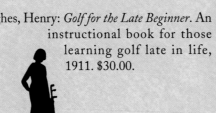

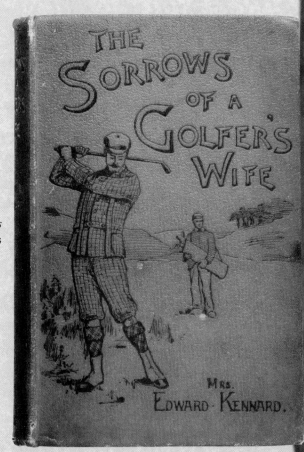

Kennard, Mrs. Edward: *Sorrows of a Golfer's Wife*. Golfing stories from a wife's perspective, 1896. $400.00.

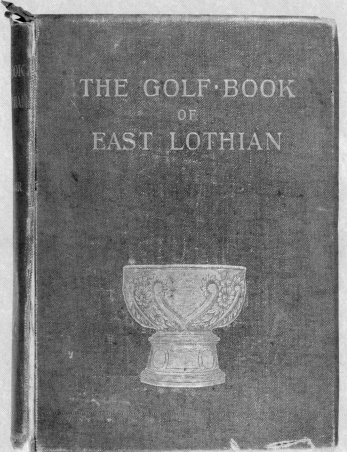

Kerr, Rev. John: *Golf Book of East Lothian*. Descriptions and historical information on the ancient courses to the east of Edinburgh, Scotland, 1896. $1,600.00.

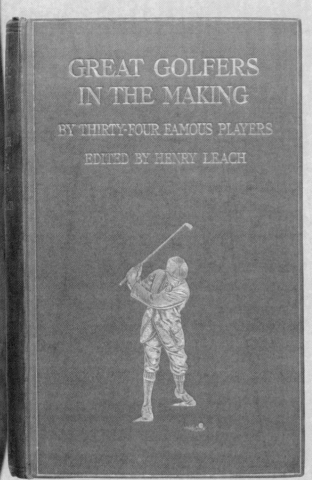

Leach, Henry, ed.: *Great Golfers in the Making*. Autobiographical accounts from 34 famous golfers, 1907. $100.00.

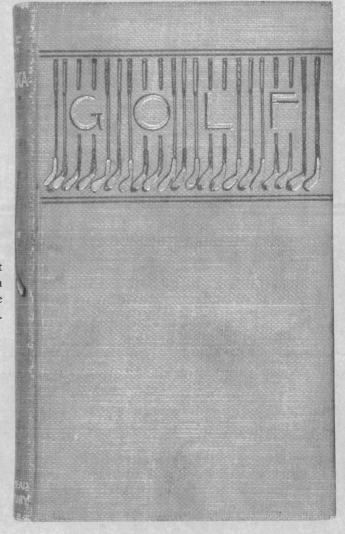

Lee, James P.: *Golf in America*. The first book about golf published in America, this is the cornerstone of American golf literature. 1895. $1,000.00.

Pearson, I., and Pascoe, A. B.; edited by Mackern, L., and Boys, N.: *Our Lady of the Green: A Book of Ladies Golf*. Overview of turn-of-the-century ladies' golf, 1899. $850.00.

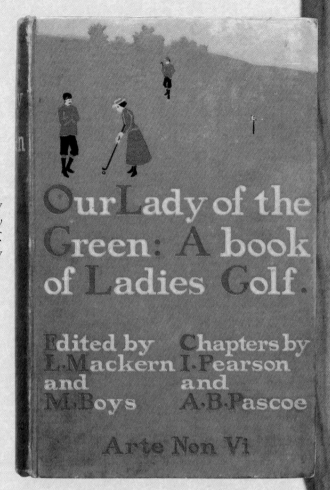

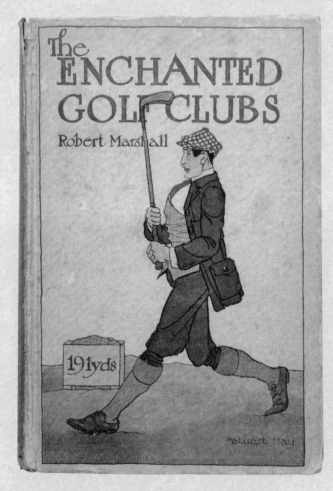

Marshall, Robert: *The Enchanted Golf Clubs*. This is the American edition of an earlier British book titled *The Haunted Major* (1902). Golf fiction, 1920. $35.00.

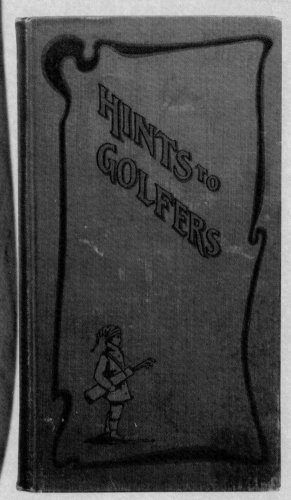

Niblick (Hanks, Charles Stedman): *Hints to Golfers*. An early instruction book written in America, 1902. $65.00.

Ouimet, Francis: *A Game of Golf.* Reminiscences by the first amateur to win the US Open, 1932. $30.00.

Ralston, William: *North Again, Golfing This Time*. Fictional accounts of gentlemen on a golf trip, 1894. $125.00.

Revell, Alexander H.: *The Pro and Con of Golf*. Philosophical essays on the game, 1915. $60.00.

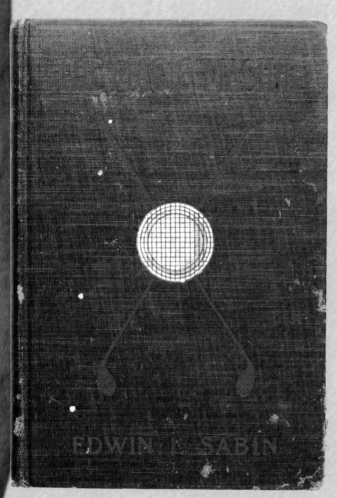

Sabin, Edwin L.: *The Magic Mashie.*
A collection of golfing stories,
1902. $75.00.

Sutphen, W. G. van Tassel: *The Golfer's
Alphabet.* Cartoons relating golf
to each letter in the alphabet.
Drawings by A. B. Frost,
1898. $500.00.

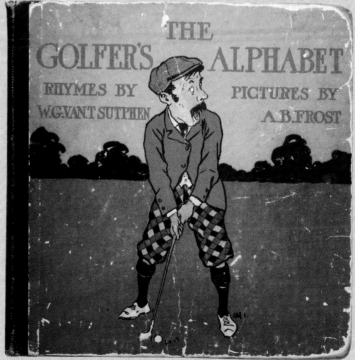

Taylor, J. H.: *Taylor on Golf*. Instruction from the five-time winner of the Open Championship, 1902. $75.00.

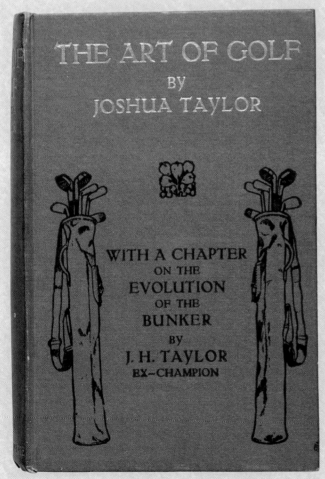

Taylor, Joshua: *The Art of Golf*. Instruction from the younger brother of the celebrated champion, who contributed a chapter, 1913. Josh Taylor was also a golf professional. $35.00.

Thomas, Jr., George C.: *Golf Architecture in America*. Architecture books, especially older titles, are in demand. 1927. $150.00.

Travers, Jerome D.: *Travers' Golf Book.* The biography of America's future 1915 US Open Champion, an amateur, 1913. $125.00.

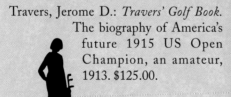

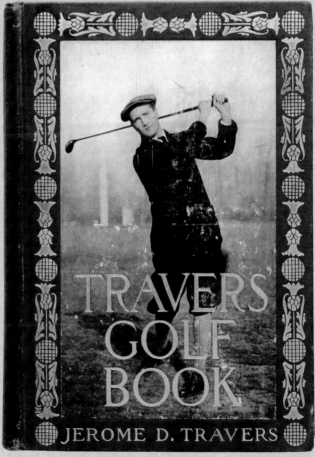

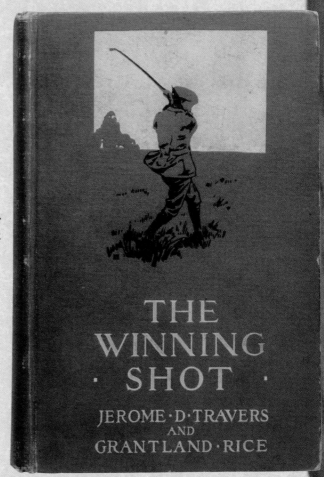

Travers, Jerome D., and Rice, Grantland: *The Winning Shot*. A historical look at Travers's best moments, 1915. $40.00.

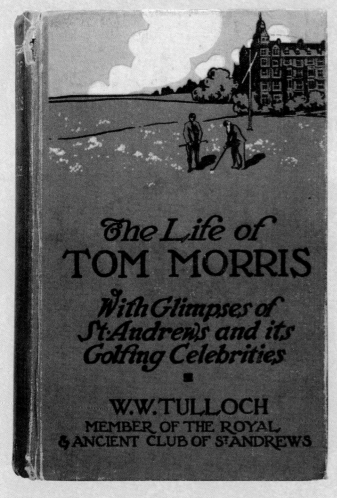

Tulloch, W. W.: *The Life of Tom Morris*. Biographical history of golf's most celebrated figure, with a large amount of St. Andrews history included, 1908. $1,250.00.

Vaile, P. A.: *The Soul of Golf.* An instructional volume, 1912. $40.00.

Victim (D.W.C. Falls): *An A.B.C. of Golf.* This rare 1898 book of humor is bound with red cord in burlap covers and has only 28 pages. $1,750.00.

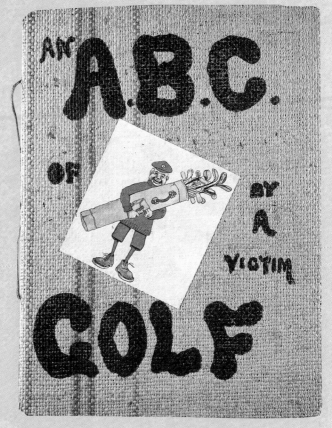

Wodehouse, P. G.: *The Clicking of Cuthbert*. Wodehouse's second anthology of golf stories, featuring "Sundered Hearts" and "The Long Hole," 1922. $25.00 without dust jacket, $250.00 with dust jacket.

Wodehouse, P. G.: *Divots*. A collection of golf-themed short stories including "The Magic Plus Fours" and "Rodney Fails to Qualify," 1926. $25.00 without dust jacket, $300.00 with dust jacket.

Wodehouse, P. G.: *Heart of a Goof*. The American published version of *Divots*, 1927. $25.00 without dust jacket, $250.00 with dust jacket.

Wodehouse, P. G.: *Wodehouse on Golf*. A collection of golf stories from previous anthologies, 1940. $40.00 without dust jacket, $250.00 with dust jacket.

One area within golf book collecting that interests many book collectors is club history collecting. Often, when a club reaches a centennial mark, its history is written and published as part of its centennial celebration. Clubs also often start recording their histories earlier than the century mark, so they can capture information that may be lost over a longer interval. It is not unusual to find histories written at fifty years or seventy-five years.

Histories from the most important clubs around the world are always targets for history collectors by virtue of the fact that they often have information concerning the more significant events in golf. But other, lesser-known clubs frequently produce history books for their own memberships, sometimes with a few extras produced for nonmembers. Some are well written and well produced and are sought after by golf book collectors.

Crail Golfing Society is one of the oldest clubs in the world, dating from 1786, and it is the only club of age that possesses all of its original minute books. This bicentenary edition club history is in two volumes in slipcase. The club is located in the town of Crail, about 15 miles south of St. Andrews in Scotland. $250.00.

OLD MANCHESTER GOLF CLUB 1818-1988

BY JEAN M. RUSSELL

Old Manchester Golf Club, Manchester, England, was founded in 1818 and published this history on the observance of its 170th birthday. Like most club histories, it was privately published and is difficult to locate outside its own neighborhood. This edition is in softcover. $60.00.

A HISTORY OF THE BRUNTSFIELD
ALLIED GOLF CLUB 1856-1996

The Clubmakers'
Golf Club

Philip Knowles

Foreword by
Alex Hay

The Bruntsfield Allied Golf Club was one of the clubs without course that shared use of the City of Edinburgh's Bruntsfield Links. This volume, in a limited edition of 600, was published on the 140th anniversary of the club's founding. $100.00.

Canadian clubs can't be overlooked, since several of them are the oldest in North America. Toronto Golf Club celebrated its centennial in 1976 with this 128-page history. $75.00.

The Toronto
Golf Club
1876-1976

One of America's earliest clubs, and one of the first clubs to be formed in the southern states was Palmetto, in Aiken, South Carolina. This volume was professionally produced for the club by the Donning Company publishers in 1992. $50.00.

The Essex County Club, Manchester-by-the-Sea, Massachusetts, was founded in 1893 and commissioned this history for its 100th anniversary. However, the book wasn't released or copyrighted until 1995. The club had a long and rich history, and the book's pages are shared by stories of golf activities as well as tennis stories. $100.00.

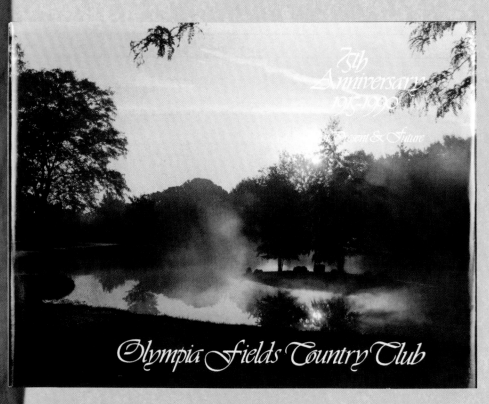

Olympia Fields Country Club, Olympia Fields, Illinois, was once the largest club in the United States, with four full 18-hole courses. It has twice hosted the US Open Championship, and it produced this historical volume in 1990 for its 75th year. $40.00.

PROGRAMS, BOOKLETS, AND OTHER BOUND GOLF ITEMS

A subset of books, this group of items includes mostly pamphlets, booklets, golf programs, magazines, and other ephemeral items of multiple pages that may not have as much permanence as a bound book. Some of these were printed in the nineteenth century and are often from very small print runs, making them rare and valuable, especially if the subject matter is important to the history of the game in some way.

Magazines with covers depicting golfers, especially nongolf magazines like *Time*, *Life*, *Newsweek*, etc., are collectible and are doubly so if they are autographed by the person on the cover. Issue number one of a golf magazine will also always be a favorite with collectors.

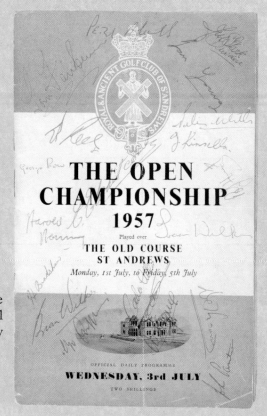

Open Championship program book, St. Andrews, 1957. The person attending the championship collected several dozen players' autographs on the cover. Bobby Locke was the Open winner. $500.00.

Open Championship program book, Carnoustie, 1968. This was the last Carnoustie Open until that course rejoined the rota in 1999. Gary Player was the winner. $400.00.

Open Championship program book, St. Andrews, 1970. Jack Nicklaus won the first of his two St. Andrews Opens this year. $400.00.

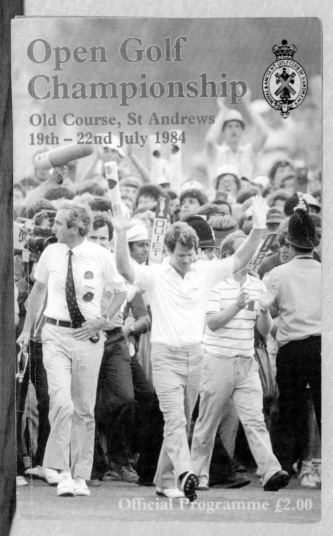

Open Championship program book, St. Andrews, 1984. Seve Ballesteros won the event; Tom Watson is pictured on the cover. $150.00.

The official program from the National Open for Miniature Golf. The event was accompanied by its association trade fair. Even in the 1930s, miniature golf had a large following. $35.00.

Bobby Jones "Flicker" books containing progressive photos of Jones swinging a driver and a mashie (one on each side of the page) in the first book, then a brassie and an iron in the second book. The effect was to see Jones in action, as though watching a minimovie. (Collectors should understand that there are replica reprints available of these Flicker books.) $250.00 each for the originals.

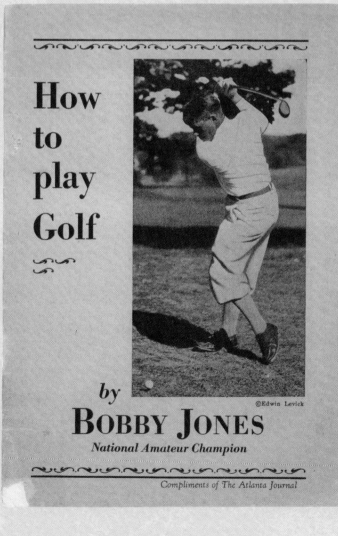

The *Atlanta Journal* produced this golf instructional book, aimed at youngsters, in the 1920s. Then, as it is now, anything with Jones's image on it was guaranteed to attract attention. $150.00.

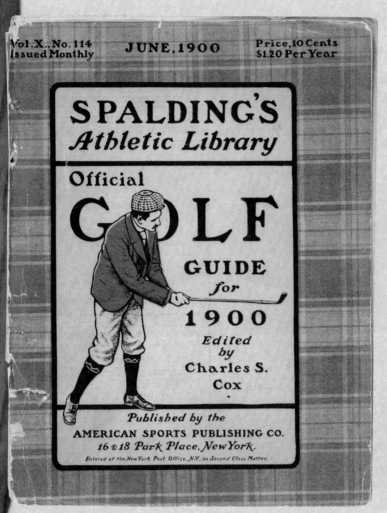

The *Official Golf Guide for 1900*, from the Spalding Athletic Library. Spalding was America's largest sporting goods dealer and produced this library for all the sports for which it sold equipment. It contained stories and biographies from the golf world, but also had many advertisements for the clubs, balls, and related golf items it sold. The ads are very valuable to collectors. $200.00.

Golf equipment catalog from the Eagrow Company of Milwaukee, vintage 1920s. This firm produced Ampco brand golf clubs made from Ampco metal, a nonrusting bronze-like alloy. $75.00.

Golf Rules at a Glance. This small booklet covered the major rules encounters that a golfer might have on any given day. It is also marked "The Oakley Golf Club, Local Rules, 1901." $125.00.

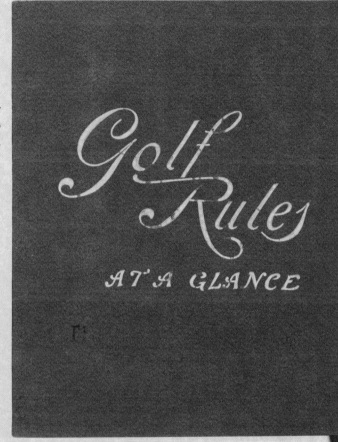

The Rules of Golf, Wilson Handy Vest Pocket Edition. The Wilson sporting goods company used this complimentary item to get people involved in golf. $65.00.

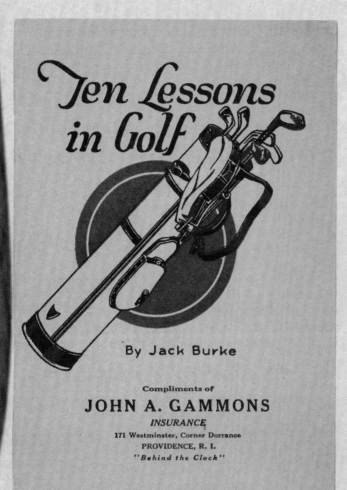

This small booklet on golf instruction was a discretionary giveaway from a local insurance agency. Written by Jack Burke. This sort of pamphlet or booklet was often discarded and is rare today. $40.00.

The Diehl-Vardon how-to booklet was a short but comprehensive look at golf for the beginning player, with photos showing how to play the game. This booklet may have been the only time Tom Vardon got higher billing than Bobby Jones. $50.00.

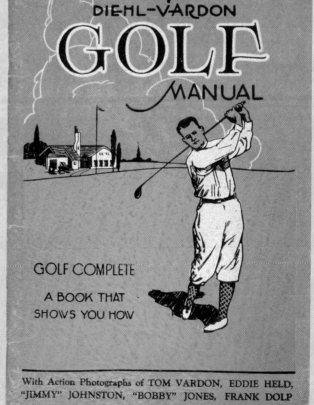

Before there was a PGA of America, regional associations for professionals existed in some areas. This 1905 directory of the Western Professional Golfers Association is a rare piece of American golf history; a lot of this sort of membership information was discarded after the formation of the PGA in 1916. $100.00.

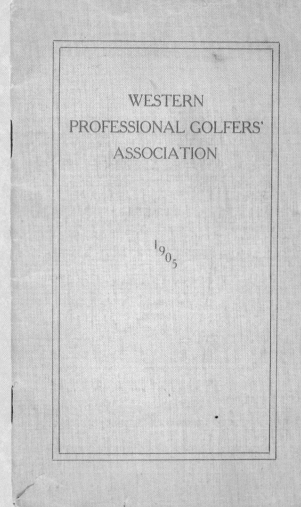

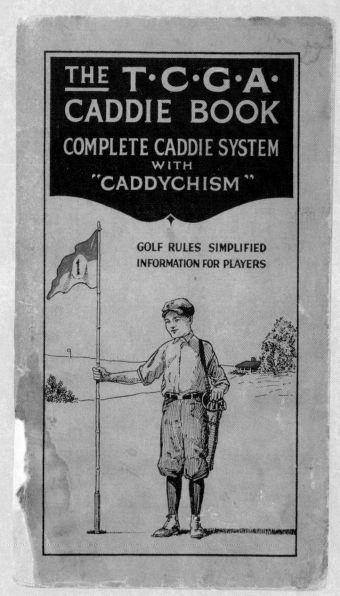

Likewise, caddie information is also an unusual find from this period, since much caddie instruction was done verbally at the individual clubs. $50.00.

In its own right, holiday advertising information from Pinehurst, North Carolina, has a collector following. Two of the resort pursuits — golf and horseback riding — are depicted on the cover of this brochure, probably from the 1930s. $50.00.

A bit more whimsical is the cover of this booklet from Pinehurst, playing on golf's ancient Scottish origins. Founded in 1895, the Pinehurst resort became a golfer's paradise in the 1920s, when it boasted 72 holes of golf. $25.00.

Weekly golf periodicals first started in Britain in 1890. The picture-rich magazine month-lies appeared after 1900 and became popular in the 1930s. The same *Golf Digest* we read today in the United States started in 1949. This number, vol. 2 #2, Spring 1950, shows the relative simplicity of the early publications. $55.00.

COMIC BOOKS

Comic books are actually periodicals, like magazines, because most of the characters/titles came out on a regular schedule. But unlike many of the other staple-bound booklets and pamphlets, the value of comics to a golf collector is the cover artwork; the pictures are usually visual sight gags without any relationship to the stories inside the covers.

Abbot & Costello, June, #9, 12¢. $4.00.

Action Comics, August 1946, #99, 10¢, Superman. $35.00.

Andy Panda, April – June, 10¢.
$6.00.

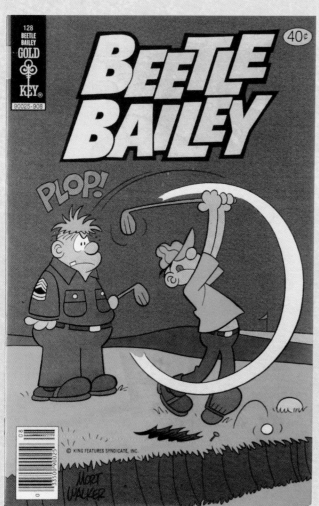

Beetle Bailey, #128, 40¢ (has UPC code).
$2.00.

Bob Hope, November, #41, 10¢, late 1950s. $10.00.

Bugs Bunny, 25¢. $3.00.

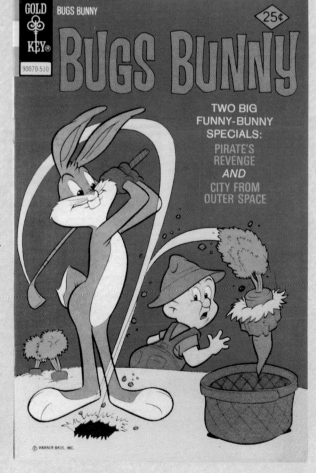

A Date with Judy, Oct. – Nov., #43, 10¢.
$6.00.

Famous Funnies, anthology, #1,
10¢. $25.00.

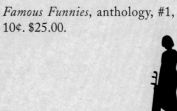

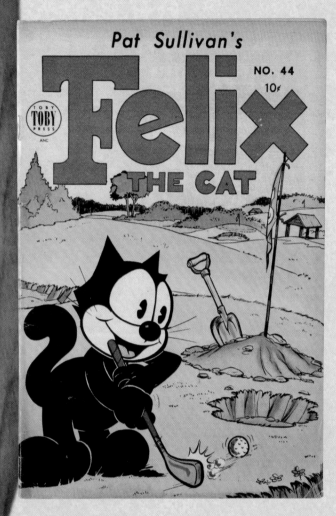

Felix the Cat, #44, 10¢, mid-
1950s. $12.00.

First Love Illustrated, January, #60,
10¢. $5.00.

The Fox and the Crow, April – May, #9, 10¢. $20.00.

Gay Comics, April, #37, 10¢, with Millie, Tessie, Nellie. $10.00.

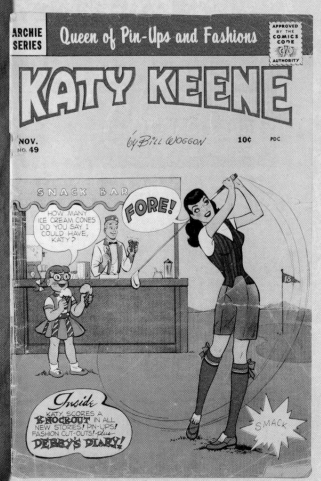

Katy Keene Comics, November, #49, 10¢ ("Queen of Pin-Ups and Fashions," "Archie Series"). $8.00.

King Comics, December, #44, 10¢, featuring Popeye and Little King. $50.00.

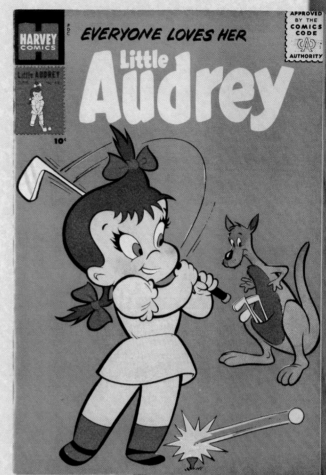

Little Audrey, June, #48, 10¢.
$4.00.

Little Ike, #2, 10¢.
$15.00.

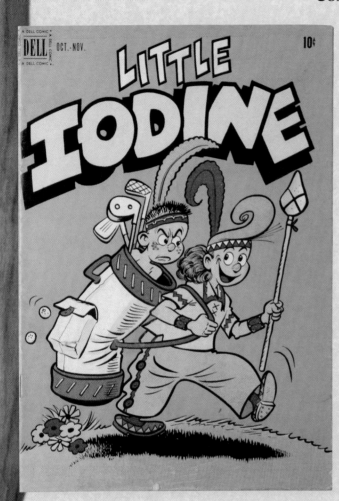

Little Iodine, Oct. – Nov., 10¢. $7.00.

Little Lotta, March, #82, 12¢, late 1960s. $4.00.

Little Max ("A Joe Palooka Magazine"),
August, #30, 10¢. $5.00.

Mickey Mouse Magazine, November 1938, vol. 4 #2,
10¢. $20.00.

Nancy, #63, 10¢.
$20.00.

EPHEMERA (PAPER)

"From the smallest, most disposal prone bits of paper like ticket stubs and scorecards to priceless prints and engravings, the full history of golf can be found printed on paper."

Ephemera, in the collecting context, is loosely defined as anything on paper (not books, not prints). There are certain niche collecting areas like photographs or cigarette cards that are quite broad.

Sheet music is one of the niche collecting areas that is affordable. Sheet music is easy to store and provides some brilliant golf artwork. Depending on age and artistic content of the cover, pieces of sheet music generally cost between $5.00 and $100.00.

CIGARETTE CARDS

The top row of three cards is from the Faulkner's Grenadier Cigarettes series. It shows golfing figures in comical interpretations of well-know golf phrases. The bottom row of three is from Ogden's Guinea Gold series. It shows three of the finest golfers from the late nineteenth century, J. L. Low, Old Tom Morris, and Horace Hutchinson. It is interesting to note that Low and Hutchinson were amateurs. Faulkner cards: $40.00 – 50.00 each. Ogden's series: Old Tom, $150.00; Low and Hutchinson, $65.00 each.

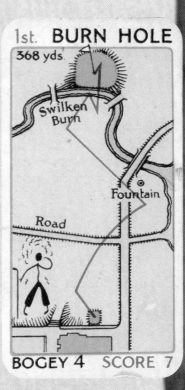

As cigarette cards go, this was a different approach. Titled "Can You Beat Bogey at St. Andrews?" it shows the first hole of the Old Course at St. Andrews, and an imaginary player has just shot a seven. Three versions of each hole (55 cards in all) were printed, so that collectors could get more cards and work at lowering the collective score — buying more cigarettes in the process. From the Churchman Tobacco Company in the 1930s. $10.00 – 20.00 each.

OLD PHOTOGRAPHS

Photos of the three greatest British golfers of the early 1900s, J. H. Taylor, Harry Vardon, and James Braid, known as the Great Triumvirate. These photos were probably framed at one time; there are traces of adhesive around the borders. $100.00 each.

Every club had a group photo taken every so often, sometimes on a special occasion when an exhibition match was scheduled or a special visitor was entertained. This 7" x 11" photo on board is of the Hesketh Golf Club, Lancashire, England (now the Stockport G.C.), taken in 1896. The group may very well have gathered for a special event, because the shortest of the three men standing in the back row against the window is John Ball, the first amateur to win the Open Championship (1890). $350.00.

The Yale University golf team of 1898. Although organized golf had been played less than a decade in the United States, one of its earliest footholds was on Ivy League campuses. Yale was the intercollegiate team champion in 1897, 1898 (splitting with Harvard in a year when two tournaments were played), and 1902 before running off an unprecedented nine in a row from 1905 to 1913. 5" x 7". $150.00.

An unknown group of English club men in front of its clubhouse, circa 1910. Undated photos are often put into an acceptable range of years based on the dress and the style of clubs in the image. This group also has a celebrity in its midst — six-time Open Champion Harry Vardon, second row, far right. $150.00.

This snapshot is probably of a holiday maker enjoying a round of golf, taken as a souvenir of his vacation. It is only 2¼" x 2¼", and the clubs look to be about 1905 to 1910 vintage. $45.00.

These two landscape-style photos show players on a golf course in the Bournemouth area. They probably hung in the clubhouse in past years. Scenes like this are interesting because they show small details of golf a century ago: the length of the grass on the putting green, the condition of the rough, the small standard in the hole instead of a flag, and the bag of clubs held by the caddie. Circa 1905, 8" x 6". $45.00 each.

A sepia-tone snapshot of golf fans, including the great Scottish singer Harry Lauder, watching while J. H. Taylor drives from the teeing ground. Photos like this, which show both an entertainer and a sports personality, have interest for two separate markets and are worth more than a snapshot of only one famous person. $75.00.

Five monochrome photos of golfers from the 1950s and 1960s, including one of the young Jack Nicklaus. Jack, $30.00; others, $15.00 each.

This advertising broadside was an early form of in-shop promotion for golf balls made by the London firm of Anderson, Anderson & Anderson. Without a lot of pizzazz, it simply listed testimonials and endorsements from publications (left column) and well-known players (right column), including Harry Everard, James Braid, and R. W. "Bob" Kirk. The size is 11" x 15", but part of the top may be missing. In-store advertising in this large size is rare, especially from 1898. $250.00.

GOLF BALLS.

SEE THAT EVERY BOX BEARS THIS TRADE MARK.

GOLF BALLS.

SEE THAT EVERY BOX BEARS THIS TRADE MARK.

ANDERSON, ANDERSON & ANDERSON, LTD., INDIA RUBBER MANUFACTURERS.
35, ST. PAUL'S CHURCHYARD, E.C.

1903

THIS CARD IS 6 INCHES LONG

Edgewater Golf Club

SELF *Chester S Horton*

OPPONENT

HOLES			Self 1ST	Self 2ND	Opp't 1ST	Opp't 2ND
	Bogey					
1 THE START	5	400 Yds.	4	4		
2 The Meadows	4	280 Yds.	4	4		
3 OLD HOME	4	265 Yds.	4	3		
4 SUNSET	3	167 Yds.	3	3		
5 THE BIRCHES	6	593 Yds.	6	5		
6 RAILROAD	5	387 Yds.	5	4		
7 Bowling Alley	5	328 Yds.	4	3		
8 THE OAKS	5	344 Yds.	4	4		
9 THE FINISH	5	367 Yds.	4	4		
	42	3131 Yds.				
TOTAL,			38	34		
HANDICAP,						
NET,				72		
SCORER	*C. M. R.*					

A scorecard with a pencil date of 1903 — old as far as scorecards go — from Edgewater Golf Club on the north side of Chicago. Chester Horton was a professional in the Chicago area for many years, beginning around 1900. Edgewater was the club where future Open and Amateur champion Chick Evans caddied as a boy. $125.00.

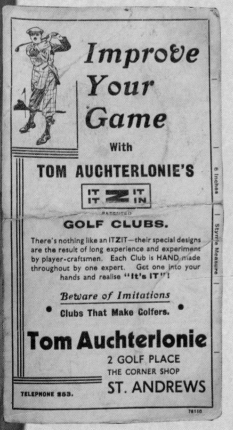

Advertising on scorecards was adopted early. The Tom Auchterlonie shop gave away these cards to visitors from out of town who were playing the St. Andrews courses. Since Auchterlonie's "Itz It" brand clubs were introduced in 1926, this card cannot be any older than that. Also note the stymie measure along the right edge of the face of the card. The card itself is 6" long — the unit of measure in declaring a stymie. Early scorecards are not easy to find, because they were one of the most expendable of all golf items. $35.00.

	OLD COURSE				NEW COURSE				EDEN COURSE		
Hole	Yds.	Par	Score	Hole	Yds.	Par	Score	Hole	Yds.	Par	Score
1	368	4		1	304	4		1	350	4	
2	401	4		2	334	4		2	420	4	
3	356	4		3	516	5		3	180	3	
4	427	4		4	333	4		4	470	5	
5	530	5		5	150	3		5	420	4	
6	367	4		6	452	5		6	330	4	
7	352	4		7	337	4		7	150	3	
8	150	3		8	495	5		8	380	4	
9	306	4		9	223	3		9	350	4	
10	312	4		10	467	4		10	430	4	
11	164	3		11	332	4		11	420	4	
12	314	4		12	482	5		12	380	4	
13	410	4		13	156	3		13	260	4	
14	527	5		14	380	4		14	180	3	
15	409	4		15	327	4		15	510	5	
16	348	4		16	417	4		16	180	3	
17	467	5		17	323	4		17	390	4	
18	364	4		18	389	4		18	350	4	
	6572	73			6417	73			6150	70	
	S.S.S. 75				S.S.S. 77				S.S.S. 73		

Marker

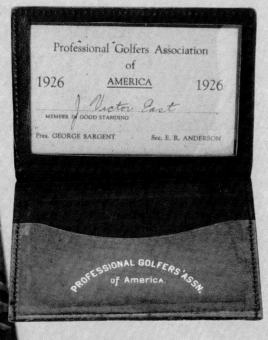

The 1926 PGA membership card of J. Victor East, the Scottish-born professional who helped to found the Australian PGA and later designed clubs for the Spalding and Wilson companies. The card is mounted in a business card case stamped with the name of the PGA of America. $250.00.

A receipt from a golfer entering a professional golf tournament in New Orleans. Golf has come a long way since 1944, when the total prize purse for a tournament was $5,000.00 and the entry fee was $5.00. 2 ½" x 4" $35.00.

$5,000 NEW ORLEANS OPEN GOLF TOURNAMENT

February 25-28, 1944

Registration Fee $5.00

PVT Joe Hine line

Two paper passes to the Greater Greensboro Open, dated 1942 and 1947. Notice how the terminology changed from "participant" to "contestant" in five years. The jugate button was a classier contestant identification than the paper tags, and the Tam O' Shanter Country Club in Chicago was one of the country's most prestigious. Private Joe Hineline, a G.I. aspiring to be a professional golfer, never fulfilled his dream. He died in combat in France later in 1944. GGO paper contestant passes, $20.00 each; jugate contestant button, $35.00.

Modern-era spectator badges from golf tournaments make a colorful display. Even though they are only a few years old, Masters practice-round tickets are sought by collectors. Containing holograms to prevent counterfeiting, they were first issued in 1995. By contrast, the US Open ticket is simpler in its design. Masters practice-round tickets, $10.00 – 15.00 each; US Open paper tickets 1990 – 2005, $5.00 – 15.00 each.

Assorted recent plastic badges from tournaments also make an interesting tour through time. Early badges from important tournaments can bring up to $40.00 or $50.00. These, from the last 15 years, are generally available for $5.00 to $15.00, except for Ryder Cup badges, which are generally a bit higher.

There isn't much of a market for golf matchbooks, whether from an important tournament or a well-known golf club, but they are colorful and fun to accumulate. Matches from the Open Championship should bring $3.00 – 5.00 for the earlier years. For those unlucky collectors who may never get into the clubhouse at Augusta National or the other elite private clubs, matches at $1.00 a book (preferably fully intact without missing match-sticks) are not a bad deal.

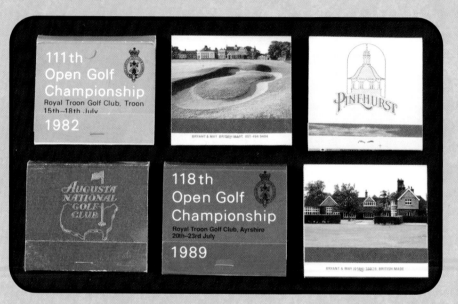

GOLF BALLS
ALL MAKES
THOUSANDS TO CHOOSE FROM
5C Each
and UP
GOLF CLUBS AND BAGS AT LOWEST PRICES
CHICAGO GOLF BALL CO., Inc.
4443 Broadway
LOOP STORE
33 West Jackson Boulevard

A business or trade card advertising the Chicago Golf Ball Company, circa 1910. $20.00.

Cigarette silks were free premiums that came with a pack of cigarettes, much as cigarette cards were distributed in the early part of the twentieth century. This series of silks featured a wide range of colleges and universities, including the Ivy League schools, the University of Chicago, the old Big 10, and many other major state universities.

Stanford University silk, $50.00.

University of Missouri silk, $40.00.

Brown University silk, $40.00.

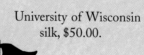

University of Wisconsin silk, $50.00.

POSTCARDS

Postcards are another collecting area in which golf collectors seeking golf memorabilia collide with geographical collectors acquiring memorabilia of anything — including golf courses — from their regions, and with other specialized collectors. The best cards are very costly, but the thousands of others less historic are very affordable and can be made into broad-based, colorful collections.

These three colored postcards from the period from 1900 to 1910 were typical for their day — featuring celebrities in a time when there was no colored print media — but are now rare gems for golf collectors. Even the monochrome or sepia cards of famous golfers from that period are valuable, but the colored cards are very special.

"J. H. Taylor Driving" (Taylor had five Open victories), $150.00.
"Vardon Pitching" (Vardon had six Open victories), $200.00.
　　"Tom Morris" (the Grand Old Man of Golf), $400.00.

Caldeno Links, Delaware Water Gap, Pennsylvania. This lovely old photographic scene of golfers shows ladies playing in long skirts, with young boys caddying. The handwritten message is appropriate: "I have become a golf fiend. Simple life will never agree with me again. May." Cancellation dated 1907. $25.00.

Illustrated golfing lady in white. Circa 1905. $10.00.

Golfing lady in red jacket, also showing a heart-shaped hole marker. Copyright 1905, New York. $10.00.

A sepia-tone card with two views of the Spalding factory in Chicopee, Massachusetts, from around 1900. $75.00.

Cape Fear Golf Links, Wilmington, North Carolina, is a club that was founded before 1900. This card was cancelled in 1931, with the card still showing play on sand greens. $5.00.

A Valentine card for the older set, with a man and caddie playing golf. Circa 1910. $20.00.

VALENTINE GREETINGS

You strike all day and fret and fuss
While caddies laugh as you do fuss.

A JOYOUS XMAS

A Christmas postcard with a golf theme. A young golfing boy with clubs, in a plaid frame. $20.00.

The artwork was by Lance Thackeray and the piece, done in 1908, was originally called "Her First Lesson." The legend, "A Quiet Game at Wolstanton," was printed for that club; any other club could have its name inserted by the printer. $35.00.

A Quiet Game at Wolstanton

THE GAME OF GOLF.
Its rather difficult

Another Thackeray illustration from the same series, showing two golfers and two caddies leaving the tee, then hunting for a lost ball. $35.00.

From a different card series, Thackeray takes a humorous shot at a lady golfer who thinks she can barely manage to pull the flagstick. $40.00.

Many cards were printed that showed the frustrations of the game. The red-jacketed golfers were a copy of the figures of the well-known artist Victor Venner. $25.00.

A golfing lout accidentally striking a gentleman was the sort of humor that was conveyed to those uninitiated in the ways of golf by early cards like this 1905 copyright piece. $35.00.

This card came from a series of some sort and is titled "Scottish Sports, Golf." $20.00.

Charles Crombie's illustrations portraying the rules of golf have been reproduced in virtually every medium — cards, prints, books, and china. $40.00.

A humorous cartoon featuring a huge hat, meant to be sent to friends from tourists. $15.00.

The railroad lines advertised golf holidays and destinations with regularity. The LNER line, which served the east coast of Scotland, touted over 600 courses at its destinations. This image is taken from one of its station-mounted posters. $10.00.

Advertising was also done with post cards. Springvale Kite golf balls were promoted here. $50.00.

The king of the magazine illustrators, Harrison Fisher, frequently drew attractive women. This image, titled "Two Up," also appeared on the cover of *Ladies' Home Journal*. 1909. $35.00.

TWO UP

A photo postcard shows a young lady with clubs and bag. Judging by the attire and equipment, the photo was taken around 1910 or afterward. $20.00.

This photo card has been hand tinted to include some color. It is a personality card showing the film star Gladys Cooper as a golfer. $25.00.

Gladys Cooper

Zeese-Wilkinson copyrighted this scene of courtship on the links in 1909. $20.00.

The boyfriend-girlfriend theme was common in golf cards. This Italian card from the 1930s shows a couple of young kids. $20.00.

The eternally silent comic strip character Henry gets involved in this golf-themed card, but not by playing golf. He's ready to play marbles on the green. $45.00.

Humiliation on the links is another common theme on postcards. The game is not easy and that fact is easily shared. $15.00.

Another calamity on the links portrayed on a card from the early part of the century. $20.00.

Judging by the number of children portrayed on post cards, golf was sweeping through the ranks of school-age kids. Copyrighted by J. Tully, 1906. $20.00.

Sonny is a bonny boy
A game of golf he does enjoy.

This hand-colored photo with motto was typical of a card that could be mailed with good wishes. Circa 1905. $20.00.

POSTAGE STAMPS

A surprising number of countries have issued postage stamps with themes of golf or golfers. These stamps can be collected as stamps by themselves, on artwork cover envelopes or on envelopes with special cancellations from golf events. Some special envelopes observe golf events but don't include golf stamps.

Collecting golf stamps and golf-themed covers has several advantages. Stamp collections don't occupy much space and can be easily stored. The artistic value of the stamps and covers makes them ideal for display when framed, and from an economic standpoint, collecting stamps and covers is one of the relatively less expensive ways to pursue a golf collection.

There is a considerable amount of history reflected with golf stamps, as seen with the cover from the opening day of Augusta National in 1933. Back in the 1880s, a friend of Old Tom Morris sent a letter to Tom by simply addressing it to "The Misser of Short Putts, St. Andrews, Fife." It was delivered on time to Tom's door. Now *that* would be a great collectible to have in a collection of golf stamps and covers.

A first flight cover, celebrating a new air mail route from Camden, South Carolina, in 1932. The stamped cachet shows sporting figures from Camden — a polo player and a golfer. $25.00.

Commemorative cover with cachet showing a golfer swinging, celebrating twenty years of airmail service from Augusta, Georgia, 1938. $20.00.

Commemorative cover with cachet announcing the opening of the Robert T. (Bobby) Jones Course, Augusta National Golf Club, January, 1933. The likeness of Jones isn't great, but it's close enough. $125.00.

The same cachet, now incorporated into a cover mailed from the 1977 Masters Golf Tournament. $15.00.

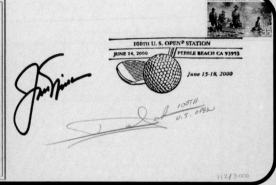

From the 100th United States Open Golf Championship, June 2000, at Pebble Beach Golf Links, California, a cachet cover saluting Jack Nicklaus (a four-time US Open Champion) and signed by Jack as well as by the designer of the cover's artwork, Delgado. $65.00.

From the same tournament, another cover with different artwork showing scenes of the course, also signed by Nicklaus. $50.00.

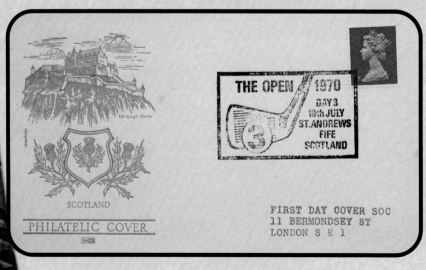

Commemorative cover from the 1970 Open Championship at St. Andrews, Scotland, where Jack Nicklaus beat Doug Sanders in a playoff. The postmark shows the cover was mailed the third day of the tournament. The two-color cachet envelope is a generic Scottish envelope with scenes of Edinburgh Castle and thistles. $35.00.

A colorful cover mailed from the World Golf Hall of Fame in (at that time) Pinehurst, North Carolina, and bearing likenesses of (Robert T.) Bobby Jones, Jr., and Babe Zaharias (Didrickson) as well as the two postage stamps issued in their honor. $40.00.

A commemorative cover with special postmark, from the 1977 Ryder Cup matches held at Royal Lytham & St. Annes, England. It was the last convincing victory the United States would see before the British team became the British and European Team, aggressively challenging the United States. $25.00.

A first-day cover from Jamaica for the issuance of a set of stamps commemorating sports and sights on the island. The set includes a golf stamp. $15.00.

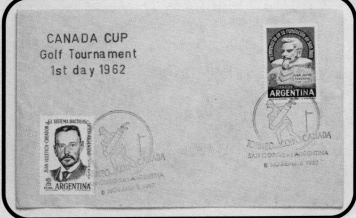

This interesting cover was mailed to observe the Canada Cup in 1962 but was posted from Argentina with special Argentinian golf cancellations. $25.00.

SILVER

"Besides religion, there is no other structured activity in the civilized world that has been celebrated in so many art forms as golf."

SILVER

Silver, both in sterling and in plate, was a medium used for artistic purposes much more in the nineteenth century than it is today. Many golf-related pieces were given as awards and trophies at club competitions, but they were useful as well as attractive.

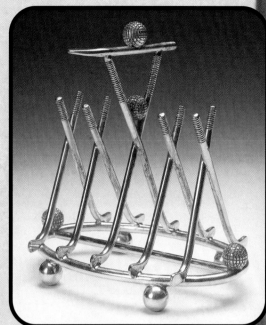

One piece of silverware that belongs in any collection is the quintessential British toast rack. By the very nature of its construction, it lends itself to being made in the image of golf clubs. There are different sizes — four slices or six — and such racks are made in sterling as well as plate. This example is hallmarked and is especially well proportioned. $400.00.

Items, especially in silver, for the desks of gentlemen golfers were frequently given as competition prizes at golf clubs. This inkwell is adorned with crossed clubs and ball. $200.00.

One of the necessities for the kit of a Scottish golfer was a flask for that wee nip when out on a chilly windswept seaside course. This silver flask has a relief design of a golfer during follow-through. $250.00.

Serving pieces were also given as prizes, but less frequently. Utilizing the mesh pattern, the balls of this ensemble are salt and pepper shakers resting on a tray. It is an unusual item and is fairly uncommon. $250.00.

New York jeweler Theodore Starr's ad shows that the ever-increasing country clubs in 1898 were in need of silver prizes for their competitions.

CLUB Committees and individuals having in view the purchase of prizes for Golfing are invited to inspect the many suitable pieces of Solid Silverware offered by this house.

THE OPPORTUNITY TO SUBMIT SPECIAL DESIGNS IS SOLICITED.
APPLY FOR ILLUSTRATED BOOKLET.

THEODORE B. STARR

206 FIFTH AVENUE   MADISON SQUARE   NEW YORK

Most golfers try to preserve their first hole-in-one ball as a keepsake and reminder of the thousands of shots taken before one finally landed in the cup. It is not unusual for the individual golfer's hole-in-one pedestal to be made from silver. This piece is dated 1932, and the ace was recorded on a 249-yard hole — pretty impressive. The clubs securing the ball and the plaque on the base are sterling silver and the hallmarks are visible. The base has a legend stating that this award was presented to the golfer by the Silvertown Ball Company. $225.00.

SILVER TROPHIES

Trophies, especially silver trophies, are collectible for a variety of reasons:

• The trophy may have been won by someone significant in the golf world.

• It may have been presented at an important event or at a famous course.

• The form may be particularly attractive.

• The trophy may contain a large amount of pure silver.

Additionally, many older trophies, if not meeting any of the preceding criteria, are now being cleaned up and recycled for prizes in current golf competitions.

 Dated 1964, this trophy is not yet an antique, but it has a very pleasant form and looks impressive. $100.00.

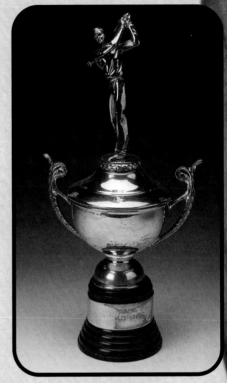

 Functional pieces also made elegant trophies, like this English silver ewer decorated with a gold medallion featuring a golfer in the old St. Andrews swing. $600.00.

A sterling silver goblet, beaker, or tumbler that has fancy decoration around the rim and was used as a trophy for a golf association tournament. Most attractive is the light engraving on the body of the goblet, which shows golfers at their game. $300.00.

The artistic side of golf collectibles is very broad. Many etchings, lithographs, and prints exist of course landscapes, golfers in action, candid scenes, and historic moments.

Most collectors use framed prints to highlight golf within their homes; the prints go along with other pieces they collect.

EDINBURGH

EDINBURGH.

THIS city, the capital of Scotland, is situated in Mid-Lothian, long. 3° W. and lat. 56° N. near the southern bank of the river Forth. The castle, an object of prime consideration, was, before the use of artillery, deemed impregnable, and is said to have been built about 617, by Edwin, one of the Saxon kings, whose territories reached to the Frith of Forth, and who gave his name to EDINBURGH, as it certainly did not fall into the hands of the Scots till the reign of Indulphus, who flourished about the year 950. The town was built for the benefit of protection from the castle, and a more inconvenient situation for a capital can hardly be imagined. The High Street, which is on the ridge of a hill, runs east and west. The castle not only overlooks the city, its environs, gardens, the new town, and a fine rich neighbouring country, but commands a most extensive prospect of the river Forth, the shipping, the opposite coast of Fife, and even some hills at the distance of 40 or 50 miles, which border upon the Highlands.

Facing the castle, down the High Street, at a mile distance, stands the abbey or rather palace of Holyrood House, built by David I. in 1128, and so named by him in memory, it is said, of his deliverance from an enraged hart, by the miraculous interposition of a cross from Heaven. This monastery he gave to the canons regular of St. Augustine, to whom, with other gifts, he granted the privilege of creating a borough between the town of EDINBURGH and the church of Holyrood House. From these canons it had the name of Canongate, which it still retains.

An hospital, commonly called Heriot's Work, founded by George Heriot, goldsmith to James VI. stands to the southwest of the castle in a noble situation, and is the finest and most regular specimen that Inigo Jones has left us of his Gothic manner. It was built for the maintenance and education of poor children belonging to the citizens and tradesmen of EDINBURGH, and is seen at the right hand of this View, which is taken from the goff ground on the Burntfield Links.

The High Church of EDINBURGH, called that of St. Giles, was supposed to have been built before the year 854; but it is now divided into four churches, and a room where the General Assembly sits. The churches and other edifices of the city, erected before the Union, contain little but what is common. Its modern edifices, however, such as its university, exchange, public offices, hospitals, bridges, &c. demonstrate the improved taste of the Scots in their public works.

The university of EDINBURGH is in very high estimation; the Professor's chairs are all filled with men of acknowledged ability; and no place ranks so high for the study of medicine.

Parallel to the city of EDINBURGH, on the north, a new town is begun, upon a plan which does honour to the present age. The city is governed by a lord provost, four bailies, a dean of guild, and a treasurer, annually chosen from the common council. The revenues of the city consist chiefly in a tax on Scotch ale, the product of which (though falling lightly on the people, being only two-thirds of a farthing on two English quarts) has been sufficient to defray the expense of supplying the city with excellent water, erecting reservoirs, enlarging the harbour of Leith, and completing other public works.

The population of EDINBURGH is estimated at from 80,000 to 90,000 persons. Its distance from London is 393 miles, N. N. W. The manufactures carried on are chiefly linen, cambrics, and paper; and its markets are plentifully supplied with all sorts of provisions. It sends one member to Parliament. The present representative is the Right Hon. Henry Dundas.

A very, very early view (image 6½" x 5") of the city of Edinburgh, engraved by J. Walker, May 1, 1798. Hand colored, the piece distinctly shows the castle and golfers and their attendants on Bruntsfield Links playing the game. Taken from an unknown book, possibly *The Itinerant*, the text provides several paragraphs of facts about the Scottish capitol city, including the population (80,000 – 90,000), and it also includes the passage "from the goff ground on the Burntfield [sic] Links." Eighteenth-century literature and artwork describing golf are both very rare. $500.00.

PRINTS

TOM MORRIS

A set of three lithographs (image size 8" x 6"), taken from an unknown book, portraying the three greatest golfers of the mid-nineteenth century: Tom Morris, Sr., is shown with club addressing the ball; his son, Tommy Morris (Tom, Jr.), poses wearing the original Open Champion's prize, "the belt," that he won three times in succession (1868 – 1870) and was thus privileged to keep forever; and Allan Robertson, the first person alleged to be able to make a living playing golf, poses with clubs. Set of three, $450.00.

TOMMY MORRIS

ALLAN ROBERTSON

A very small (5" x 4") original pen-and-ink cartoon drawn by "Lary," a cartoonist whose work, which included this piece, frequently appeared in the pages of *Punch Magazine*. $125.00.

CERAMICS & GLASS

One of mankind's earliest art forms was decorated pottery. As golf became a popular pastime, golf themes quickly appeared on all manner of ceramics and glassware. Many of the most handsome pieces, like bowls, cups, vases, and mugs, were produced to be used, in large part, as trophies and awards for different club competitions. Many more decorative pieces simply carried forward the theme of the links for those who enjoyed partaking in the new sport.

Collectors will find that the oldest ceramic items, from the turn of the century, were artistic masterpieces from such noteworthy companies as Wedgewood, Spode, Lenox, and Rookwood. Today they dominate this segment of collectibles, with prices frequently in the four figures. However, there are many items of more recent vintage that are affordable collectibles bringing grace, color, and often a little humor to any display.

Two almost identical Lenox (US) Ware beer steins depicting golfers in dark green, one with a gold rim, the other with a silver rim. The accuracy of image, deep color, and quality firing make Lenox pieces highly sought. Similar Lenox pieces come in other forms and colors. Range: $800.00 – 1,000.00 each.

The unmistakable black background with female figure on this piece of Wedgewood Kenlock Ware (England) makes it easy to identify. This rare creamer dates from the early 1900s. $750.00 – 1,000.00.

Water pitchers from the 1890s made by Minton (Staffordshire, England), with golf caricatures. Range: $400.00 – 500.00 each.

One of the most popular patterns to collect is the Royal Doulton series depicting stylized old golfers. Made for many years, a wide variety of pieces exist. Here a pitcher with lid, a tapered vase, a candlestick, and a lidded container for sugar (or mustard) represent a small portion of the range of sizes and shapes. Also produced were a great many bowls, cups, plates, platters, and serving pieces. Smaller pieces can be bought for $100.00 or less; larger serving bowls and platters often go for over $1,000.00. Pitcher, $350.00; vase, $500.00; candlestick, $300.00; sugar bowl, $300.00.

Gerz (Germany) stoneware water jug, gray with blue highlight glaze. This producer made only a handful of golf-related pieces around the turn of the century. $400.00.

A ceramic trade advertising piece, likely meant to sit on a shelf in a pub or perhaps on the bar itself, promoting Plus Four brand whiskey (England or Scotland). These pieces are unusual and hard to find. $400.00.

A tobacco humidor with metal cover, made by Wiltshaw & Robinson (Staffordshire, England) as part of its Carlton Ware line, probably early twentieth century. Although the company began making golf pieces before 1900, some were made as recently as the mid-1950s. $250.00.

A leaded glass beer stein with pewter lid. The mug portion is hand painted with a golfer and trees. Circa 1910. $300.00.

The cream and tan color combination on this coffee mug was typical of that on many Lambeth Doulton pieces. The Doulton studio that produced these relief pieces was located in the Lambeth district of London. $300.00.

The distinctive blue background on this piece with relief golfers is a hallmark of the W.T. Copeland & Sons (Staffordshire, England) Copeland Spode line. This milk pitcher dates from the early 1900s. $450.00.

Even children's china was available in golfing themes. Royal Doulton produced the well-known Bunnykins series in the 1930s. This cereal or pudding bowl was one of many table pieces in the series. $250.00.

Teddy bears were another favorite with children. Entire children's tea sets in this pattern were sold. The beverage beaker or tumbler is marked for Elijah Cotton, Lt., Hanley, Staffordshire (England). Tumbler, $200.00; 7" plate, $125.00.

This mug in amber and brown came from the Dartmouth Pottery (Dartmouth, England) in the 1940s. $100.00.

Mugs like this were given away with purchases of cooking flour in the 1930s. The pieces were produced by the Sleepyeye Indian tribe in Wisconsin. Other similar pieces included bowls, cups, and jugs. $60.00.

Golf-themed cocktail sets were very popular up until World War II. This blue glass decanter with silver appliqué of a golfer came with four small glasses with silver-edged rims and dates from the 1930s. $250.00.

A set of two spirits bottles in wooden rack. They are of amber color in the three-sided "pinch" shape and have applied silver details. One is labeled "Scotch," the other "Rye." $150.00.

A clear glass paperweight containing a ceramic dimple golf ball. $50.00.

A glass box with lid upon which is etched a golfer dressed in 1940s style. It might have been on a desk in order to hold cigarettes, matches, buttons, or coins or something else similar. $30.00.

A commemorative plate depicting Old Tom Morris, specially made for the 1990 Open Championship at St. Andrews. With presentation box, $75.00.

Ceramic figure of a stylized caddie or golfer, seated in front of a green holding a ball. $25.00.

Ceramic whiskey bottle in the shape of a golfer bent over flask. The inscription reads "The Nineteenth Hole." $75.00.

Bud vase with front adornment of a golfer in exaggerated swing follow-through. $35.00.

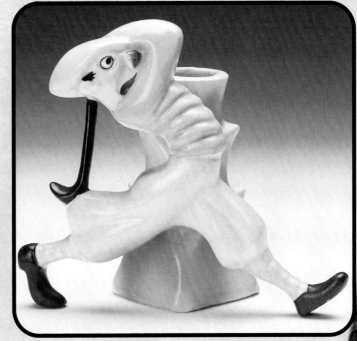

Fanciful rabbits playing golf, in ceramic. A set composed of a male and a female. $50.00.

A flower vase in the shape of a stylized tree with a male golfer swinging a club in front. $35.00.

A garden figurine of a small laughing boy caddie who almost looks Asian. $60.00.

An ashtray featuring a golf bag with plastic clubs, perhaps picks for cleaning the bowl of a pipe. Marked for Charles Millar & Son Co. $25.00.

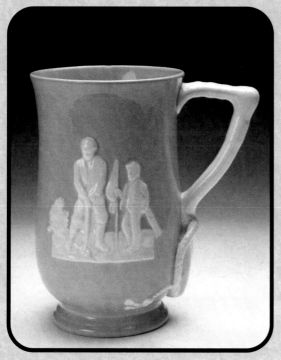

A recently made coffee cup with coloration and white relief design reminiscent of the Lambeth Doulton line. $25.00.

A figure in the style of a Hummel and with a large golf ball and four clubs. $30.00.

A vase or flower planter in the shape of a golf bag, typical of the type used for a theme floral arrangement or potted greenery delivered from the florist. $15.00.

A similar theme planter in the shape of a large golf ball with golfer adjacent. $15.00.

Ceramic coasters or ashtrays printed with pictures of golfers of the 1960s. One is marked for Mickey Wright, another for an older Gene Sarazen. These were given as extras with a half dozen Wilson K-28 golf balls. The set of four, $50.00.

JEWELRY

Like the other decorative art forms, jewelry with golf themes has been around since Victorian times. The range in values reflects the materials used. Gold or sterling silver jewelry isn't cheap, and so the material cost increases the value. There is, however, plenty of inexpensive golf jewelry to be found.

The person who had this ring and ID bracelet made probably had a lot of money, a severe golf swing defect, and a large ego. The two pieces are made from 14-karat gold and diamonds. $5,000.00 (or whatever the going rate for the gold and diamonds is).

A silver badge presented to honorary members of the Swedish Golf Union. $100.00.

This small replica golf bag is the repository for a small group of ladies' hat pins, all in a golf theme. There are several drivers made from silver, one made from glass, two clubs made from seashells, an iron club, and some golf balls. Depending on the material and workmanship, hat pins run between $35.00 and $200.00; the little golf bag, $75.00.

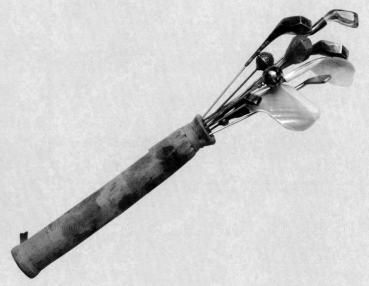

There's a little bit of kitsch in this lapel pin in bronze. $25.00.

Another lapel pin, of a golf bag with clubs. $35.00.

This assembly of pin-on items includes several types of badges. Club members' badges: from Wortley G.C., $30.00; from Broomie Knowe G.C., $35.00; from Jolly Golfer's Club, $25.00. Caddie badges: from Westchester Hills G.C., $50.00, and from Drumlins, $30.00. Lapel pins: gold golf clubs with a thistle and amethyst at the mid-point of the shaft, $175.00; three clubs in a circle, $35.00; and a small, enameled golf bag, $50.00.

Pocket watch with a golfer and caddie on its painted dial. $150.00.

METALWARES

This section is a catchall for all items made from metal excluding those pieces in sterling silver or plate, jewelry, and golf irons. Most of these pieces are household items, decorations, or pieces of whimsy. Useful and decorative items made in golf themes first appeared regularly in the 1890s in Britain and in the following decades increased in number and frequency. There are literally thousands of golf-type items in existence for collectors to find. Those that are of an early age or of high-quality workmanship are most valued by collectors. Even collectors with modest means can locate many of these objects and build a broad collection with reasonable expenditure.

The Parlor Putter smoke stand is a much sought-after collectible. It was designed to keep busy the golfer who might be housebound by bad weather or any other inability to get to the golf course. This model holds three putters and has three tunnel-like holes in the base into which a ball could be putted from the parlor carpet. Inside each hole was a metal ramp that returned the ball to the person putting. The top level of the stand holds a glass ashtray; the lower level has indentations to hold three balls.

Parlor Putters come in two varieties — a three-club, three-hole triangular arrangement and a two-hole, two-club version. Made by the Wellington-Stone Company, Chicago, most are painted red, white and green, others come in unpainted bronze. $750.00 – 1,250.00.

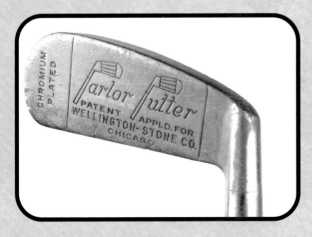

The original putters that came with the stand are as scarce, if not more rare, than the stand itself. Individual club, $200.00.

281

Bronze statue of a golfer swinging a club. The clothing is of the Bobby Jones era, the 1920s. $400.00.

Bronze statue of a golfer holding a club. The golfer's outfit is reminiscent of clothing from around 1910. $200.00.

Bronze statue of a golfer, swinging a club, attached to a desk ashtray. The clothing is indicative of pre–World War I golfers. $250.00.

Higher quality golf statuary is often cast in bronze. Items marked with a foundry name or mark are the best to have; however, where there is no identifying marking, the artistic nature of the piece helps determine value:

• Is the pose accurate? The golfer in the middle photo on this page is holding his club in a way that is not a normal position for a golfer.

• Is the figure properly scaled and proportionally correct? Often the golf club itself is too short or long for the size of the human.

• Is the detail of the clothing, especially in the act of swinging, true to life?

Bronze figure of a caddie mounted on a raised wooden base. The detail is not nearly as fine as on more expensive pieces. $60.00.

Small metal statue of the "Dunlop Man." The Dunlop Golf Company, manufacturer of rubber tires, and subsequently rubber golf balls, would provide these small statues as displays to club professionals who sold Dunlop balls in their shops. This one is mounted on an ashtray. $500.00.

Another Dunlop Man in bronze, perched atop a large golf ball. $350.00.

The Dunlop Man is shown in this 1917 ad from *Golf Illustrated*.

This golfer in humorous pose was cast from an inexpensive metal and enameled. While the quality is not the same as that of the better bronze statues, this piece's unusual nature make it a nice collectible. $125.00.

This display piece featuring a ball and a miniature flagstick is probably a hole-in-one award. $75.00.

A simpler hole-in-one piece features a small bronze base with three prongs for holding the golfer's ball with which he scored the ace. On the base, there is a banner on which the golfer's name has been inscribed. $50.00.

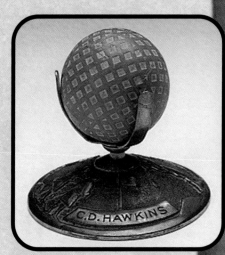

These are two items that utilize the form of the golf ball. The bottle opener/can opener has a dimple ball for a handle. The bronze paperweight is topped with a mesh-pattern ball, the sort of which went out of favor in the 1930s. Bottle opener, $15.00; paperweight, $50.00.

The mesh-pattern ball in the center of this ashtray turns it from a fairly pedestrian piece into a golf collectible. $25.00.

Two similar cast-iron doorstops of a gentleman in plus fours playing golf. This is one of the more common golf-themed doorstops, but finding one with original paint (left) is difficult. This particular model has also been reproduced, and modern copies (below) can readily be found. In original condition, $200.00 – 300.00; reproduction, $30.00.

Cast-iron doorstop of gentleman in plus fours at the top of his backswing, circa 1920 and with original paint. $300.00.

Unpainted bronze doorstop of a shouting caddie. This one is a little more modern than the painted items. $150.00.

Cast-iron doorstop depicting a short caddy struggling with a large golf bag. This particular item is difficult to find. $400.00.

Bronze bookend with a relief image of an unhappy caddie, along with the legend "Profanity." $100.00.

Pewter beer stein set with a silver medallion of a golfer swinging a club. Circa 1920s. $150.00.

Pewter beer stein decorated with raised relief crossed golf clubs and ball. Circa 1960s. $35.00.

A sheet-metal biscuit tin with painted historical golf scenes on four sides and the lid. Probably English. $200.00.

A modern sheet-metal biscuit tin that once contained Scottish shortbread fingers. Relatively modern, it features a scene of the Royal & Ancient clubhouse. As a collectible, $10.00 (though one may find something similar including the shortbread at a Scottish grocery or department store for the same price today).

A tin box with hinged lid simply decorated with an image of crossed golf clubs. It may have been a biscuit tin or a promotional item included with the purchase of the six golf balls inside. $75.00.

TOYS & GAMES

It was only logical that the children of golfers have scaled-down equipment as well as games with golf themes. Boxed golf games ranged from traditional board games to tabletop games with mechanisms that simulated hitting a small ball. The artwork on the cover of a game box may be more interesting than the game inside. Some games are a hundred years old.

Golf toys included affectations of golf clubs, indoor miniature golf sets for use on the floor, and a variety of devices that allowed kids to hit a tethered golf ball in the yard. True children's clubs, made by club makers in smaller sizes, are shown in other sections.

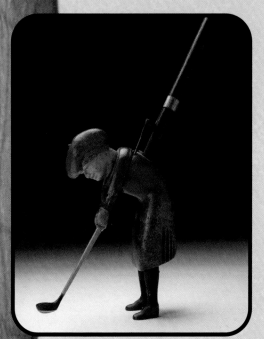

One of the most popular and unusual golf toys is the Schoenhut golfer. The player has articulated arms and is attached to a long pole, at the end of which is a trigger. When the trigger is activated, the golfer swings at the ball. The game set was composed of several figures; just having one in operating condition is a valuable find. $250.00.

The Wilson Putting Disc was a typical indoor putting aid to be used in the parlor on winter afternoons to fight off boredom. The box it came in is especially handsome. $60.00.

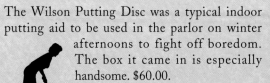

This very old child's noisemaker has nothing to do with golf except it is decorated with the image of a golfer. $30.00.

Many golf games were played with special dice, as was this number, called Galloping Golf. Some of these games can still be found on tables or bars in country club grill rooms or card rooms. Circa 1960. $50.00.

Some of the oldest golf games came in the form of playing cards. The deck of blue cards called Golfer Playing Cards had card backs with golf clubs as part of the design. They date from the early part of the twentieth century. The other deck comes in a fancy storage box decorated with a lady dressed in 1920s attire hardly suitable for a day on the links. Blue deck, $60.00; fancy boxed deck, $75.00.

This ad promoting golf cards appeared in (US) *Golf* magazine in 1898.

Standard-size playing cards, marked "Po-Do." Also marked with golf phrases. They were probably a free gift used as an incentive to buy a dozen Po-Do golf balls. Circa 1940s. $25.00.

A bridge-size boxed deck of cards bearing a drawing of Arnold Palmer playing golf. From the 1960s or early 1970s, when Arnold may have been past his playing prime but was still a huge endorsement name. $35.00.

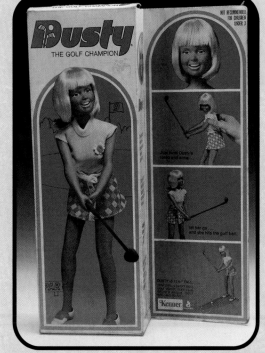

For the sports-minded young lady, the Dusty doll actually swung a golf club and hit a ball. Dusty's miniskirt golf outfit probably dates her from the late 1960s or early 1970s. Having the original box makes any collectible toy much more valuable. She is 11½" tall and was made by the Kenner Toy Company, Cincinnati, Ohio. $125.00.

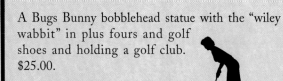

A Bugs Bunny bobblehead statue with the "wiley wabbit" in plus fours and golf shoes and holding a golf club. $25.00.

Even everyday items found around the house can have golf themes or associations. Some of these items can be the most fun to collect, because one never knows what will turn up next.

The Ri Co Muffler could have been used on any chilly day, anywhere, but a lady using it on the golf course makes for good artwork on the lid of the box. From the early part of the twentieth century, the box is an excellent display piece. $75.00.

A Zippo-style cigarette lighter embellished with a golfer hitting a ball toward a par three hole green. From the 1940s or 1950s. $50.00.

Although this lever-style cigarette lighter has lost some of its enamel decoration, the form of the golfer is still visible. $35.00.

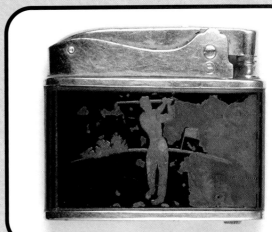

An especially ornamental cigarette lighter in the shape of a golf ball supported by a tripod of three small clubs. $75.00.

A smoker's pipe with the bowl in the shape of a dimpled golf ball. $50.00.

A desk clock in the shape of a golf ball on a pedestal. The face of the clock is marked "Ernest Borel." $75.00.

Two nice golf-themed items from a man's chest of drawers: a shoehorn decorated with a red-coated golfer and a hairbrush in silver plate and decorated with a medallion of a golfer swinging a club. The shoehorn was undoubtedly a giveaway with a golf ball purchase, since it was provided by the St. Mungo Manufacturing Co. St. Mungo was a ball company in Scotland that eventually set up an American subsidiary. Shoehorn, $100.00; hairbrush, $75.00.

A trade tin, once containing Par brand aftershave powder, with the image of a golfer on the front. Tins, especially with colorful artwork, are always appreciated by collectors. $35.00.

A set of four drink coasters with cylindrical storage box. The lid to the storage box is adorned with a golf club and has a golf ball serving as a handle. $50.00.

This ice bucket for the bar was probably sold as a potential prize for a club competition. The winner's name could be engraved on the shield-shaped escutcheon. The handle was made from two golf irons. $125.00.

This lid to this boxed set of drink coasters decorated with an Art Deco golf theme is marked "The Halle Bros. Co." $60.00.

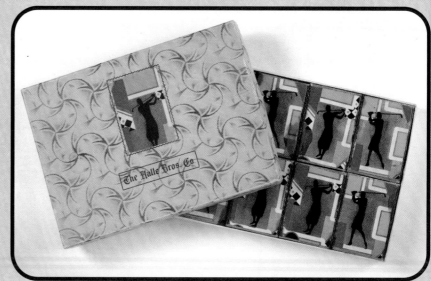

This set of spare shirt buttons was sold in a package that included a picture of a man, in a shirt, holding a golf club. The buttons are not special golf shirt buttons; the marketers used a golfing theme for the packaging. The card with buttons has been put into an Art Deco frame for display. $40.00.

Transistor radios rapidly became the rage in the early 1960s. This radio in the form of a driver head helps illustrate the variety of wireless radio forms. The crown of the club head says "Championship…7 Transistors." $50.00.

Golf figures were mostly made in metal. This caricature of a golfer with bag was carved from wood. Probably a one-of-a-kind item, it makes for an interesting golf display. $125.00.

Some collectors may classify this as kitsch, but plastic items like this very young golfer with bag of clubs are the sort of items that don't often get saved. Fifty years from now this may be a highly sought-after piece due to its scarcity. $20.00.

Golf also has its anthropomorphic side. This rabbit with clubs was intended to delight young children. $20.00.

Similarly, this rubber duck with golf clubs was probably a favorite around bath time. $25.00.

The Kitchen Sink

There is so much golf-related material to collect that it will not all fit neatly into categories. Here are some odds and ends that help to show the breadth and depth of golf materials that can be collected. They truly include everything except, perhaps, the kitchen sink.

Blazer badge for members of the U.S. National Golf Association at its Senior Open. $25.00.

Blazer badge for officials of the World Series of Golf Tournament, Akron, Ohio. $50.00.

The highest level of achievement within the PGA of America is the Master Professional. This is the blazer badge the Master Professional is permitted to wear. $50.00.

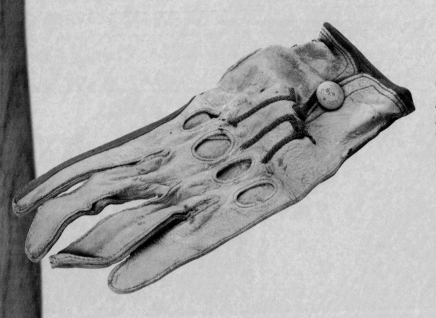

Gloves specifically designed to be worn for playing golf were first used in the 1890s. This full-fingered glove probably was made in the 1930s or early 1940s and was sold through the New York firm of Harry C. Lee & Co. $20.00.

This ad from 1900 shows golf gloves are not a recent innovation.

FOWNES

GOLFING GLOVES
For Men and Women

FOWNES

This medallion was issued by the German Golf Association in 1938, shortly before the start of hostilities in the Second World War. $200.00.

A necktie holder for a gentleman's closet, displaying the image of a 1930s or 1940s golfer. $25.00.

These five leather bookmarks were made by the late Bill Mortland, who collected the steel name stamps professionals used to stamp their names on the clubs they made and sold. He'd decorate the leather strips with the stamps and give them to his friends. $10.00 each.

Hole flags from US Open championships and other professional tournaments are generally sold at those events. Range $25.00 – 60.00, depending on age — those for the older events are more scarce. Autographed by the winner, $100.00.

COLLECTOR BOOKS
informing today's collector

www.collectorbooks.com

For over two decades we have been keeping collectors informed on trends and values in all fields of antiques and collectibles.

This is only a partial listing of the books on antiques that are available from Collector Books. All books are well illustrated and contain current values. Most of these books are available from your local bookseller, antique dealer, or public library. If you are unable to locate certain titles in your area, you may order by mail from **COLLECTOR BOOKS**, P.O. Box 3009, Paducah, KY 42002-3009. Customers with Visa, Master Card, or Discover may phone in orders from 7:00a.m. to 5:00 p.m. CT, Monday – Friday, toll free **1-800-626-5420**, or online at **www.collectorbooks.com**. Add $4.00 for postage for the first book ordered and 50¢ for each additional book. Include item number, title, and price when ordering. Allow 14 to 21 days for delivery.

1-800-626-5420 Fax: 1-270-898-8890

www.collectorbooks.com